Media Pasts and Futures

CRITICAL, DIGITAL AND SOCIAL MEDIA STUDIES

Series Editor: Christian Fuchs

The peer-reviewed book series edited by Christian Fuchs publishes books that critically study the role of the internet and digital and social media in society. Titles analyse how power structures, digital capitalism, ideology and social struggles shape and are shaped by digital and social media. They use and develop critical theory discussing the political relevance and implications of studied topics. The series is a theoretical forum for internet and social media research for books using methods and theories that challenge digital positivism; it also seeks to explore digital media ethics grounded in critical social theories and philosophy.

Editorial Board

Published titles

Critical Theory of Communication: New Readings of Lukács, Adorno, Marcuse, Honneth and Habermas in the Age of the Internet
Christian Fuchs
https://doi.org/10.16997/book1

Knowledge in the Age of Digital Capitalism: An Introduction to Cognitive Materialism
Mariano Zukerfeld
https://doi.org/10.16997/book3

Politicizing Digital Space: Theory, the Internet, and Renewing Democracy
Trevor Garrison Smith
https://doi.org/10.16997/book5

Capital, State, Empire: The New American Way of Digital Warfare
Scott Timcke
https://doi.org/10.16997/book6

The Spectacle 2.0: Reading Debord in the Context of Digital Capitalism
Edited by Marco Briziarelli and Emiliana Armano
https://doi.org/10.16997/book11

The Big Data Agenda: Data Ethics and Critical Data Studies
Annika Richterich
https://doi.org/10.16997/book14

Social Capital Online: Alienation and Accumulation
Kane X. Faucher
https://doi.org/10.16997/book16

The Propaganda Model Today: Filtering Perception and Awareness
Edited by Joan Pedro-Carañana, Daniel Broudy and Jeffery Klaehn
https://doi.org/10.16997/book27

Critical Theory and Authoritarian Populism
Edited by Jeremiah Morelock
https://doi.org/10.16997/book30

Peer to Peer: The Commons Manifesto
Michel Bauwens, Vasilis Kostakis and Alex Pazaitis
https://doi.org/10.16997/book33

Bubbles and Machines: Gender, Information and Financial Crises
Micky Lee
https://doi.org/10.16997/book34

Cultural Crowdfunding: Platform Capitalism, Labour and Globalization
Edited by Vincent Rouzé
https://doi.org/10.16997/book38

The Society of the Selfie: Social Media and the Crisis of Liberal Democracy
Jeremiah Morelock and Felipe Ziotti Narita
https://doi.org/10.16997/book59

Paradoxes of Digital Disengagement: In Search of the Opt-Out Button
Adi Kuntsman and Esperanza Miyake
https://doi.org/10.16997/book61

Digital Platforms and Algorithmic Subjectivities
Edited by Emiliana Armano, Marco Briziarelli and Elisabetta Risi
https://doi.org/10.16997/book54

Forthcoming

Digital and Social Media in Africa
Edited by Henri-Count Evans, Ruth Teer-Tomaselli and Tinashe Mawere

Critical Communication: A Memoir
Vincent Mosco

The Left and Digital Politics: Political Parties from Platform Neoliberalism to Platform Socialism
Marco Guglielmo

Critique of the Political Economy of the Media
Manfred Knoche

Media Pasts and Futures

Critical Reflections on
Power Without Responsibility

EDITED BY

DES FREEDMAN AND
MICHAEL KLONTZAS

University of Westminster Press
www.uwestminsterpress.co.uk

Published by
University of Westminster Press
115 New Cavendish Street
London W1W 6UW
www.uwestminsterpress.co.uk

This book first published 2025

Cover design: www.ketchup-productions.co.uk
Series cover concept: Mina Bach (minabach.co.uk)
Print and digital versions typeset by Newgen North America LLC

978-1-915445-64-3 paperback
978-1-915445-66-7 epub
DOI: https://doi.org/10.16997/book74

Suggested citation: Freedman, D. and Klontzas, M. (eds.), 2025.
Media Pasts And Futures: Critical Reflections On Power Without Responsibility
London: University of Westminster Press.
DOI: https://doi.org/10.16997/book74
License: CC-BY-NC-ND 4.0

To read the free, open access version of this book online,
visit https://doi.org/10.16997/book74
or scan this QR code with your mobile device.

CONTENTS

Part II Market Impoverishment

Part III Media Reform: Democratic Choices

Part IV Public Interest: A Historical and Contemporary Analysis

CHAPTER 1

Introduction

Des Freedman and Michael Klontzas

Media have changed the world but, crucially, the world has changed the media.

That interaction lies at the heart of this collection of essays that aims to provide fresh analyses of both historical trends and pressing issues affecting media landscapes across the globe. These include discussions of the emergence of the 'free press' in a range of countries, the structural dynamics of media industries from Latin America to East Asia, the dangers to public discourse posed by the increasing concentration and marketisation of media and tech industries, the role and definition of publics in media production and consumption, the possibilities of radical journalism, and the prospects for the democratic reform of our communications systems.

The collection takes as its inspiration James Curran and Jean Seaton's *Power Without Responsibility*,[1] a highly influential historical account of press, broadcasting and the internet that is focused on the UK but which has both predictive power and global ramifications. First published in 1981, *PWR* is—at the time of writing—shortly to have its ninth edition, testimony to the quality of its rich empirical content as well as its major contribution to policy debates on and public understanding of press regulation, public service broadcasting and the online world. It traces, in great detail and in vivid prose, major trends in the development of the UK media including: the industrialisation and 'moral decline' of the British press; the origins of public service broadcasting; the relationship between television and public taste; the media's role in the 'making' and 'remaking' of British cultural life; and the political and social consequences of digital growth.

One of *PWR*'s greatest qualities is its determination to confront some very well-established shibboleths of media history including the notions that:

- advertising liberated the press from government control;
- the campaign to abolish newspaper taxes in the first half of the 19th century was motivated by a commitment to freedom;
- the radical press in the second half of the 19th century declined because of a lack of support;
- the era of 'press barons' is no longer with us;
- the UK has always had a robust and competitive newspaper market;
- newsrooms have always been beacons of editorial independence;
- media influence is harmless;
- the press has consistently held power to account;
- the BBC was designed to be the 'voice of the people';
- the BBC was always able to rise above 'politics';
- the introduction of commercial television 'dumbed down' British broadcasting;
- there was a perennial Conservative consensus to destroy the BBC;
- the internet has equalised society.

There may be nuggets of truth in all these claims—as with many other 'common sense' assumptions and stereotypes—but *PWR*'s strength is to challenge them and to make visible the often hidden story that the British media have long played an important role in reproducing establishment power and setting the limits of the 'ethic of consensus' (*PWR*, 256) that dominates broadcast journalism. As Simon Frith pointed out in his review of the first edition of *PWR*, Curran and Seaton's 'starting point is that the media serve "the interests and ideology of capital"' (Frith 1982, 140)—in other words that the press, broadcasting and the internet are both expressions *and* drivers of wider social relations, rather than being seen as depoliticised or solely through a technological lens as they so often are.

PWR is thus a curious and rather wonderful mixture of textbook and manifesto. At one level, it provides students, researchers and general readers with an encyclopaedic guide to the provenance of media systems, institutions and theories that are often seen as 'taken for granted'. However, it is also an *intervention*: not quite a 'call to arms' but a firm reminder that the content, platforms and data that saturate our lives are inscribed with particular histories and politics that mean that they are never set in stone, never impermeable to challenges, always dependent on context and susceptible to change. *PWR* is, above all, an elegant and passionate reminder that media systems are neither predictable nor immutable but the product of a noisy and volatile environment populated by a range of different actors including aggressive capitalists, authoritarian bosses, radical journalists, conformist editors, self-interested politicians and combative audiences.

Indeed, *PWR* contains a lively internal political dialogue between authors who may share the same commitment to the vision of a fearless and independent media but who have rather different perspectives on the limitations and possibilities of the specific media they are writing about. Curran's chapters on the commercialisation of the press, the rise of newspaper moguls, the moral degradation of journalism (epitomised by the phone-hacking scandal of 2010) and the libertarian perspectives of internet gurus, are lacerating in their condemnation of the abuses of private power and establishment failures over the last 200 years. Seaton's chapters on broadcasting history are more circumspect in their criticism; they have a more sympathetic assessment of the rise of radio and the BBC followed by the impact of television on the national imagination, reflecting what she sees as the more positive role public service broadcasting has played in mediating between government and citizenry than has been the case for an unregulated and often uncontrollable commercial press system.

While Curran is determined to puncture the myths of 'liberal' press history and to explore the negative consequences of a commercial logic, Seaton appears to have a more likeable research subject: a broadcast culture that has long been regulated and orientated towards the notion of 'public interest' in a manner alien to the highly partisan British press. So, while Curran focuses on the ethical failures of and diminishing trust in newspapers, Seaton is significantly more optimistic about the legacy and quality of British broadcast culture. ITV, the UK's first commercial television network was (at least in its early days) 'an energizing, populist force which gave expression to working-class culture' (257) while '[l]ike the British Raj, the BBC combined privilege and moral purpose' (257). Despite mounting criticism in recent years for the BBC's role as an instrument of elite power (see, for example, Mills 2016 and Freedman 2019), she describes the Corporation as 'an imperfect beauty' (337) and a 'national treasure and world resource' (339) that has become 'one of the world's great objectivity traders' (342). Public service, therefore, is a contradictory beast: capable of innovation, representation and dialogue at the same time as containing political dissent and fostering the interests of the establishment. As Seaton herself writes: 'Public service can perhaps only be measured by what it is institutions agonise over. If you are only there to make a profit, everything is far simpler' (347).

This combination of a highly critical assessment of the limitations of market power and a more favourable historical account of a public-minded project resonates with John Durham Peters' description in this volume of Curran and Seaton's 'social democratic' vision of the media. According to Simon Frith, in his review of *PWR*:

> Curran and Seaton are social democrats rather than Marxists. They explain the media's ideological effects in terms of imperfect competition. The political solution is state intervention in the media market place. The democratic task is to ensure that other interests besides big capital can make their voices heard. (Frith 1982, 140-141)

At a time of entrenched neoliberal values and repeated attacks by pro-market governments on redistributive projects and public provision of society's resources, a social democratic vision like this now appears as particularly refreshing and almost radical, perhaps explaining the enduring relevance and popularity of *PWR* as a text that offers both sharp analysis of, and much-needed prescriptions for the ailments of contemporary media and technology. How, otherwise, can we even imagine a press that is not subservient to the whims of media moguls, and consider defending public spaces against the rapid encroachment of the market?

This collection emerged from a series of workshops organised in 2022 by the Goldsmiths Leverhulme Media Research Centre and hosted by the Communication and Media Research Institute at the University of Westminster (the two institutions at which Curran and Seaton are respectively based). These seminars brought together a diverse range of leading scholars and practitioners to address selected themes drawn from *PWR*. Speakers were encouraged to use Curran and Seaton's book as their starting point—to summarise and critically assess its claims—but more importantly to evaluate its continued relevance by extending the analysis to their own experiences as academics and media professionals drawn from a range of countries across the globe.

These contributions form the basis of the chapters presented in this collection. We have organised the chapters into five sections, all of which directly speak to the core concerns of *PWR*. The book starts with a series of **comparative international overviews** which reflect on the relevance of *PWR* for media scholarship in countries including Japan, the US and India. The section on **market impoverishment** draws directly on *PWR*'s critique of the limitations of corporate ownership and commercial imperatives in delivering a representative or democratic media system and includes assessments of contemporary branded content industries, the Australian news market, Brazilian journalism and the historic (and ongoing) role of telecommunications companies in the media.

The next section on **media reform and democratic choices** follows on from the final chapter of *PWR* to offer imaginative policy prescriptions for transforming the media in the public interest and to highlight ongoing campaigns both to defend public service initiatives under attack, as well as to propose the extension of democratic ideals to the digital platforms of the future.

The fourth section on **the public interest** relates directly to Jean Seaton's assessment of public service broadcasting and contains a range of contributions from Australia, Belgium and the UK that address the legacy, traditions and uncertain future of public service media as they face both hostile governments and avaricious rivals. Next, the section on **radical journalism** picks up on James Curran's groundbreaking analysis of what happened to the working-class press in the 19th century by looking at three different case studies of progressive journalism ranging from the 1820s through to the 1980s and, in relation to Black British audiences, contemporary possibilities.

The book concludes with two brand-new reflections on the origins and influences of *Power Without Responsibility* by the book's authors James Curran and Jean Seaton. Looking back as well as forward to its ninth and final edition, Seaton notes that *PWR* was, and remains, 'peculiarly positive' about the media despite the many and profound criticisms of the communications landscape that populate the book.

Power Without Responsibility is often described as a 'seminal' text in media scholarship and we have no reason to disagree with this assessment. However, the best scholarship never stands still. Just as the authors regularly update *PWR* with new editions, *PWR* itself is best read in conjunction with other 'classic' histories and critiques that see the media as vehicles through which capitalist interests were developed and maintained (e.g. Curran 2002, Garnham 1990, Herman and Chomsky 1988, Hesmondhalgh

2019, Hood 1980, Murdock and Golding 1974, Glasgow University Media Group 1976). *PWR* remains an essential starting point for any understanding of media sociology, history and politics and we hope that this edited collection of critical if appreciative essays will make a small contribution to the body of knowledge about the role and development of the media that was changed forever by the publication of *PWR* back in 1981.

Note

1 Henceforth *PWR*; all subsequent page references from the 8th edition.

References

Curran, J. 2002. *Media and Power*. Routledge.

Curran, J. and Seaton, J. 2018. *Power Without Responsibility: Press, Broadcasting and the Internet in Britain*, 8th edition. Routledge.

Freedman, D. 2019. '"Public Service" and the Journalism Crisis: Is the BBC the Answer?', *Television & New Media*, 20(3), 203–218.

Frith, S. 1982. 'Review of *Power Without Responsibility*', *British Journal of Sociology*, 33(1), 140–141.

Garnham, N. 1990. *Capitalism and Communication: Global Culture and the Economics of Information*. Sage.

Glasgow University Media Group 1976. *Bad News*. Routledge.

Herman, E. and Chomsky, N. 1989. *Manufacturing Consent: The Political Economy of the Mass Media*. Pantheon.

Hesmondhalgh, D. 2019. *The Cultural Industries*, 4th edition. Sage.

Hood, S. 1980. *On Television*. Pluto.

Mills, T. 2016. *The BBC: Myth of a Public Service*. Verso.

Murdock, G. and Golding, P. 1974. For a Political Economy of Mass Communications. In R. Miliband, and J. Saville (Eds.) *Socialist Register* (pp. 205–234). Merlin.

Part I

Comparative International and Critical Overviews

CHAPTER 2

Power Without Responsibility: A Celebration

John Durham Peters

Power Without Responsibility is a textbook in the same way that Euclid's *Elements*, probably the most influential work in the history of mathematics, is a textbook. *PWR* is also a paradigmatically central, field-defining work, and the fact that many students have read it should be seen as adding to its lustre. The book is a serious historical and analytic study and has nothing of the diluted content and bells-and-whistles glitz that are so often characteristic of introductory level textbooks in media studies. Sometimes works of history, such as Howard Zinn's *People's History of the United States* or Yuval Harari's *Sapiens*, are read as textbooks and I put *PWR* in this class, as it offers a compelling historical narrative of wide interest.

One of the key features of *PWR* is its synthetic achievement. This is a book that speaks to many different constituencies in media studies. It has been taken up by scholars working with both critical-cultural-humanistic approaches and social-scientific ones. Its synthesis is visible in part in its ability to combine two centuries of press and broadcasting history, and more recently, internet history, into a single book. But its synthesis lies not only in its materials, but in its argument. The book has always been defiant of twin orthodoxies: from the right, the progress-narrative that the press had happily grown ever more free thanks to its embedding in free-market forces, and from the left, the disdain for public service broadcasting as hopelessly timid and manipulated by elites. This is a social-democratic media history, richly based in archival sources, spiked with vignettes, and *interdisciplinary*. It is sceptical of tales of virtuous markets and critical but constructive about the possibilities of a media system that would genuinely serve the public interest. It is animated by the vision, as it states in its closing words, of 'power and responsibility exercised on behalf of the public' (*PWR*, 508). The book is also rich with policy suggestions. It has a humanistic approach without the worst kind of cultural-studies posturing, a political-economic approach without the worst kind of reductionism, and a sociological approach that is attuned to the complex interactions of market, state, class and culture. The book is the godfather of social-democratic media histories.

Power Without Responsibility is a book about Britain, but you can't write about Britain without writing about the globe. (Well, maybe you can, but you probably shouldn't!) It is not in the least an insular book. Like British media programmes, the British media system has been widely exported, emulated and studied around the world. The book is full of comparative comments from Australia to Zimbabwe, and is particularly embedded in European debates about public service broadcasting.

Some of the book's early chapters on the press in 19th-century Britain remain canonical for media historians. They show the critical role played by the radical press, and the nationwide reach of the press decades before broadcasting. *PWR*'s analysis here is subtle, looking to function rather than form in seeing the deep structural affinities between 19th-century print and 20th-century broadcasting.

The social-democratic vision of the authors is unmistakable, but they are never dogmatic and often present subtle counternarratives. Their defence of the BBC is never fawning; they call it 'an imperfect beauty' (*PWR*, 337), and note that it has no monopoly on public service broadcasting. Though they systematically debunk the laissez-faire narrative of a press liberated by markets, they also show with nuance how the market can pressure media in a more democratic direction. British newspapers started shedding their conservative politics in an effort to reach a working class with more disposable income in the 1930s (*PWR*, 61). Or, as Chapter 24 concludes: 'Keeping information honest is not a luxury: it is a matter of self-interest' (*PWR*, 443). Here the authors pick up a central tenet of free-market doctrine and turn it into an argument in favour of truth-telling journalism.

The book is particularly devastating against techno-liberationist arguments about the internet. The 1990s vision of digitally networked boutiques where everyone does their own thing as sold by Nicholas Negroponte and others Curran and Seaton show to be negated by IT corporate megaliths. They correctly peg social media as 'polarisation merchants'. If there is a weakness of the book, it would be in its inability to keep up with events. WikiLeaks is painted as a dissident, anti-state anarchic group, rather than as a pro-Russian, pro-Trump shill, for instance. Headlines change faster than books do, and if the initial lustre of the internet as a democratic force does not need to be destroyed once again here—events have already done that—it is easy to appreciate the rich and accessible introduction this book offers to the digital turn.

The writing is clear, engaging and occasionally pungent. The book offers a brisk, grounded history, with dates, acts and people. It is also informed by a genuine wisdom, such as the remark that the ultimate dividing line in the 21st century is not between East and West, rich and poor, male and female, or Islam and Christianity but 'between those who want to live together and those who do not' (*PWR*, 405–6).

When I was a visiting scholar at Goldsmiths College in 2000, I sat in on James Curran's lectures on British media history. The auditorium was packed, and he held forth with wit, intelligence and charisma. He told the students that his profit from the sale of each book was the price of a lager and invited them to join him at the end of the course in a local bar, where he would treat them all to one. Clearly this book is a labour of love. This was one of the best ways I've ever seen of treating the thorny royalty problem of assigning one's own books!

I was delighted when, in 2019, the book won the International Communication Association (ICA) Fellows Book Award, whose history was strongly tilted toward North American scholars. Recognising *Power Without Responsibility* reaffirmed the 'International' in ICA and acknowledged the absolutely central role that British scholarship has played in our field, and the absolutely central role that this book has played in British scholarship. In a moment when thinking people everywhere worry about the decline of public institutions and the hard times befalling the press, it is a gift to have a book that has been a steady beacon pointing the way toward a history and future of a democratic media system.[1]

Note

1 I thank Michael Schudson for earlier collaborations on this text.

CHAPTER 3

Using Media History to Inform Media Policy

Nelson Ribeiro

In the last four decades *Power Without Responsibility* (*PWR*) has affirmed itself as a classic book on the history, theory and politics of the media. When the first edition came out back in 1981, Curran and Seaton dared to argue against the dominant view according to which media and communication studies should be separate from history. The disinterest in the historical analysis of the media was clearly visible in the US where communication studies was mostly born out of social sciences, and the study of speech and journalism (Simonson and Park 2016). Even though the field in the UK followed a different route, emerging out of a 'symbiosis of functionalist sociology, Western Marxism and literary criticism', it also maintained a poor relation with history (Bailey 2009, xvi). In continental Europe, notwithstanding the long tradition of newspaper history, especially the German *Zeitungswissenschaft*, and the influence of semiotics, literary studies and critical theory, the final decades of the 20th century also saw media studies mostly following a sociological approach, disregarding history as an important factor. The same trend could be found in Latin America where communication studies started with the study of journalism, epistemologically tied to the humanities, but was soon influenced by the US sociological and functionalist approaches (Fuentes Navarro 2016).

The practice of studying media systems and practices without taking into consideration how these evolve and change over time—in other words, disregarding history—became prevalent during the second half of the 20th century. The separation between the two fields was also reinforced by historians who mostly ignored journalism and the media in their work (Schudson 2002), widening the gap between history and media and communication studies.

This scenario in which the two disciplines for the most part ignored each other was countered solely by a few works, of which Curran and Seaton's book is one of the most notable. The first edition immediately tied history and communication together: from the first pages of the introduction to the last chapter dedicated to proposals for the reform of the British media system. Subsequent editions underlined the authors' arguments for the strong entanglement of the two fields. The book made clear that whatever the new challenges faced by the media—whether the commercial pressures on broadcasting in the 1970s and 1980s or the advent of the internet and social media in the 1990s and 2000s—a comprehension of how media institutions and practices have changed and evolved over time is essential to understand the contemporary media landscape: the result of its history combined with the emergence of new technologies and new actors at a given time.

When the book first came out it was labelled 'polemical' (Hood 1984), not least because of its provocative title that highlighted the media's influence on society and its lack of accountability to citizens even in democratic societies. Curran and Seaton not only criticised the market during a period in which neoliberalism was prevalent on both sides of the Atlantic, they also proposed reforms to the media system, defending its role as a public service. This role is examined in their second chapter on the history of broadcasting in the UK, and in particular in their historical analysis of the BBC. By grounding their views on the media and the different proposals for media reform on extensive historical research, Curran and Seaton made a crucial contribution to blurring the boundaries that separated media studies from history, thus placing media historiography at the centre of the discussions on media policy. This was an innovative and audacious feature of the first edition, and has continued to be so in the most recent editions in which the authors also rely on historical analysis to make concrete proposals for the regulation of the present media ecosystem.

While the book has been praised for its courage in defending the role of the media while criticising its shortcomings, its role in the development of media history continues to be very much ignored. It was, however, a seminal book in this regard. *PWR* not only helped counter the historical amnesia that many found and still find in media and communication studies, but it has been extremely influential in the revival of media history. Besides arguing that present media institutions and practices are the result of a series of past events, discussions, and political and business decisions, Curran and Seaton make the case that media history needs to be brought to the fore in debates on topics such as media regulation, media ethics, public service, and press freedom and objectivity, especially if one continues to advocate the importance of independent media in democratic settings. If the need to consider history when designing policies that will shape the future media landscape remains today a contentious idea, it was far more controversial in the early 1980s, which speaks volumes of the authors' audacity in disrupting the mainstream mindset.

To fully comprehend the authors' innovative approach, one needs to consider that the concept of media history was relatively uncommon in the early 1980s (O'Malley 2002), which led Curran (1993, 27) to later consider historical research as the 'neglected grandparent of media studies'. There were a few exceptions to this—one of the most important being Michael Schudson's *Discovering the News* (1978)—and it is still in evidence today: in the absence of media history on many undergraduate and postgraduate curricula, and also in the exclusion of historical works from some of the major journals published in media and communication studies. While in some institutional settings the new field dedicated to the study of mediated communication was placed detached from the humanities and schools of social sciences, the cultural turn (Hall 1997)—by looking into the ideological effects of mediated representations—mostly focused on audiences and textual analysis. This also contributed to its ahistorical positioning (Bailey 2009).

Even though it can be argued that other canonical works, particularly those taking a comparative approach to media systems—from *Four Theories of the Press* (Siebert, Peterson and Schramm 1956) to *Comparing Media Systems* (Hallin and Mancini 2004)—also rely on history to ground the different models being proposed, *PWR* remains unique in that it openly embraces media history, placing it at the core of the argument throughout. Half of the chapters are dedicated to press and broadcasting history and even those devoted to media theory and media policy are filled with concepts and examples drawn from the study of the evolution of media technologies and audience practices. This makes the volume a distinctive work of scholarship. Today it continues to be one of the few major books to discuss media policy and theory based on a historical analysis, accounting for its impact across and beyond the English-speaking world. The authors focus on the UK media system rather than attempt to provide a global narrative encompassing different political and cultural contexts, yet this has not curtailed the book's international influence. On the contrary, it has functioned as a source of inspiration for authors writing on media history (e.g. Bourdon 2018; Ribeiro 2014; Rosa et al. 2020; Sohr 1998) and media policy in different countries across the world (e.g. Shaw 2016; Valcke and Ausloos 2014).

More than four decades after the first edition of *PWR*, and despite some scholars contending that media history has in the meanwhile achieved the status of a mainstream field of academic inquiry (Hampton 2005), it continues to be very much perceived as being on the margins of both history and communication studies. In 2008 Barbie Zelizer provided a diagnosis of the engagement between history and communications. Fifteen years later her diagnosis continues to resonate. According to Zelizer (2008, 5), 'the mainstream of communication research relates hesitantly to history' which she puts down to the fact that historical research challenges communication studies' 'primary orientation to the present and its lack of recognition that an interest in contemporary times draws boundaries around a point in the present in parallel fashion to historians' drawing of boundaries around a point in the past' (2008, 5).

Furthermore, scholarship produced by media historians tends to challenge some of the mainstream narratives driven by technological determinism (Curran 2008). By pushing back against such narratives, media history makes an important contribution to our understanding of the media. However, it may not be accepted by those within the field of communication studies who embrace the idea that new technologies signal a total disruption from the past and thus need new theories and new concepts to be explained. Nonetheless, media history is also to blame for its secondary status as a field, especially its tendency of being media specific and paying 'too much attention to the technology of communications, and too little to their content and processes' (Curran 2002, 135).

Despite all the challenges and shortcomings that media history must deal with today, the significant progress it has made in the last two decades is undeniable. *PWR* was not only a precursor of an increased interest in the historical analysis of the media, it noticeably contributed to that surge. By arguing that a comprehensive understanding of contemporary media institutions and practices cannot be fully achieved if one disregards its history, Curran and Seaton's book became one of the most influential works to not only advocate but demonstrate how media history can be placed at the core of media and communication studies and not just at its margins. This, I believe, has allowed the book to leave a significant epistemological imprint on the field.

References

Bailey, M. 2009. Editor's Introduction. In M. Bailey (Ed.), *Narrating Media History* (pp. xx–xxiv). Routledge.

Bourdon, J. 2018. The Case for the Technological Comparison in Communication History. *Communication Theory*, 28(1), 89–109.

Curran, J. 1993. Rethinking the Media as a Public Sphere. In P. Dahlgren and C. Sparks (Eds.), *Communication and Citizenship: Journalism and the Public Sphere* (pp. 27–56). Routledge.

Curran, J. 2002. Media and the Making of British Society, c.1700–2000, *Media History*, 8(2), 135–154.

Curran, J. 2008. Communication and History. In B. Zelizer (Ed.), *Explorations in Communication and History* (pp. 46–59). Routledge.

Franquet, R., Richeri, G. and Hibberd, M. 2020. The Introduction of Commercial Broadcasting in Europe. In K. Arnold, P. Preston and S. Kinnebrock (Eds.), *The Handbook of European Communication History* (pp. 257–276). Wiley Blackwell.

Fuentes-Navarro, R. 2016. Institutionalization and Internationalization of the Field of Communication Studies in Mexico and Latin America. In P. Simonson and D.W. Park (Eds.), *The International History of Communication Study* (pp. 325–345). Routledge.

Hall, S. (Ed.) 1997. *Representation: Cultural Representations and Signifying Practices.* Sage.

Hallin, D. and Mancini, P. C. 2004. *Comparing Media Systems: Three Models of Media and Politics.* Cambridge University Press.

Hampton, M. 2005. Media Studies and the Mainstreaming of Media History. *Media History*, 11(3), 239–246.

Hood, S. 1984. Book review: *Power Without Responsibility*. The Press and Broadcasting in Britain. *Media, Society & Culture*, 6, 73–74.

O'Malley, T. 2002. Media History and Media Studies: Aspects of the Development of the Study of Media History in the UK 1945–2000. *Media History*, 8(2), 155–173.

Ribeiro, N. 2014. *Salazar e a BBC na Segunda Guerra Mundial: Informação e Propaganda*. Almedina.

Schudson, M. 1978. *Discovering the News: A Social History of American Newspapers*. Basic Books.

Schudson, M. 2002. News, Public, Nation. *American Historical Review*, 17(2), 481–495.

Shaw, I. S. 2016. From Citizen Journalism to Human Rights Journalism: Framing the Ebola Epidemic in Sierra Leone on Facebook. In B. Mutsvairo (Ed.), *Participatory Politics and Citizen Journalism in a Networked Africa* (pp. 262–278). Palgrave Macmillan.

Siebert, F. S., Peterson, T. and Schramm, W. 1956. *Four Theories of the Press: The Authoritarian, Libertarian, Social Responsibility, and Soviet Communist Concepts of What the Press Should Be and Do.* University of Illinois Press.

Simonson, P. and Park, D. 2016. On the History of Communication Study. In P. Simonson and D. Park (Eds.), *The International History of Communication Study* (pp. 1–24). Routledge.

Sohr, R. 1998. *Historia y Poder de la Prensa.* Andrés Bello.

Valcke, P. and Ausloos, J. 2014. Audiovisual Media Services 3.0: (Re)defining the Scope of European Broadcasting Law in a Converging and Connected Media Environment. In K. Donders, C. Pauwels and J. Loisen (Eds.), *The Palgrave Handbook of European Media Policy* (pp. 312–328). Palgrave Macmillan.

Zelizer, B. 2008. When Disciplines Engage. In B. Zelizer (Ed.), *Explorations in Communication and History* (pp. 1–12). Routledge.

CHAPTER 4

Power Without Responsibility: The UK Legacy

Tom O'Malley

Power Without Responsibility's (*PWR*) legacy in the UK can be approached by considering its relationship to media and communication studies, critical thinking about the history of communications and to media policy studies.

Media and communication studies

UK media and communication studies emerged from a number of traditions, including research conducted in the USA and the social scientific traditions at Leicester University, the Polytechnic of Central London and Glasgow University in the 1960s and 1970s. It owed much to the influence of literary studies, inflected through Richard Hoggart and Raymond Williams and to theoretical work done at the University of Birmingham's Centre for Contemporary Cultural Studies. It was also influenced by the growth of interest in Marxist history and theory in UK higher education at the time.

Texts about and critical of the media had appeared before *PWR*. People had been writing about the press for over a hundred years; work had also been done on cinema, radio and television.

The book has a number of important characteristics which have contributed to its success in the UK. It is interdisciplinary, using history, sociology and political and social theory. It has a commitment to the idea that the media can and should be better able to serve democracy. It contains two distinct authorial voices, with different emphases. This injects an openness into the text, which is particularly useful in a teaching context.

It benefitted from, and played an important role in, the formation and development of media studies courses in the UK. In the 1980s and 1990s, when important strands within media and cultural studies stressed the diffuse nature of media influence, *PWR* retained a firm focus on power, history and policy. It stood rock solid against the tendency for some areas of media studies to be obsessed with the present at the expense of perspective. The revisions to successive editions helped teachers keep track of changes in the media environment. New editions also evidenced the speed and complexity of changes since 1981.

Finally, as far as this author knows, no book has been produced which tells the same story and deals with similar theoretical issues, from a neo-liberal or conservative perspective. Its judgments may have been challenged, but the book hasn't!

History

PWR was part of a growing interest in media history in the 1960s and 1970s, one which accelerated thereafter. Its historically grounded critique of the 'liberal' theory of press freedom has resonated. It was a timely statement of a case made before in various ways. It brought to that case new historical research which radically challenged the received view of press history. It did not provide a detailed history of the press, nor was that its aim. But the book opened up a fresh perspective on one of the central debates in UK press history. *PWR* remains a powerful challenge to any historian attempting an overarching counternarrative.

Its detailed revisions have provided a lucid narrative of recent developments in debates over press standards, regulation, power within press organisations, the relationship between politicians and the press, and the industry's continuing role in intervening in and shaping British political culture.

Broadcasting history is covered in some detail. It engages directly with attacks on the BBC and the principle of public service broadcasting (PSB) from the 1970s onwards. This advanced common understandings of the history of broadcasting, by situating them, critically, within historical and contemporary sociological thinking and providing a template for subsequent accounts. Its vigorous but not uncritical defence of PSB continues to provide a resource for thinking about the issues at a time when the very future of PSB is in doubt.

PWR has adapted this historical approach to the study of the internet. In the UK, there has been a fairly uncritical and fatalistic view of the power of the internet amongst some politicians, students, journalists, academics and members of the public. *PWR* challenges celebratory accounts of the history and nature of the internet, demonstrating that it should be understood using history and political economy—not transcendental technophilia.

Policy

PWR sets out a persuasive argument for retaining public service media and for injecting public accountability across the system.

During the 1960s and 1970s, press and broadcasting policy was a major issue on the Left, among media trade unionists, and the moral Right. The book was first published in 1981, when it was reasonable to assume that Labour would be re-elected by 1984, and that Thatcherism was a passing electoral phase. Of course, this is not how things turned out, but at the time there was a chance that progressive communication policies might be implemented by an incoming Labour administration. Eventually, a 'New Labour' government was elected in 1997 and proved unwilling to pursue progressive media reform throughout its 13 years in office.

Yet in the years since 1981, the book's arguments gained wider currency, providing ballast for the work of campaigning groups like the Campaign for Press and Broadcasting Freedom, Hacked Off, the Media Reform Coalition and Media North. These activist groups have kept alive the idea that there needs to be radical reform of media policy in the UK.

PWR has also contributed to the education of students in media policy and to a progressive current in contemporary studies of the field.

The book has also made a significant contribution to another trend in policy thinking, one which has become stronger since the 1940s. This was the idea that the state should have a role in regulating the press; that this role should not be to censor, but to enable. It also played a role in rehabilitating the idea of public service broadcasting on the Left from an earlier emphasis as a tool of the state and class domination to a much more subtle, complex reading of its role.

PWR is a textbook, a political intervention, a reassessment of old views about the press and broadcasting, a vivid synoptic critique of the internet, and an insistence on the relevance for democracies of accountability and plurality in the media. It continues to assert, strongly, the need for an informed debate about, and reform of, the media in the UK, in spite of unfavourable political circumstances.

Resources

Campaign for Press and Broadcasting Freedom: https://www.cpbf.org.uk/
Hacked Off: https://hackinginquiry.org/
Media North: http://medianorth.org.uk/
Media Reform Coalition: https://www.mediareform.org.uk/

CHAPTER 5

Irresponsible or Irrelevant? Japan's Two-tiered Journalism System

Kaori Hayashi

Almost 30 years ago, I began my graduate studies at the University of Tokyo. Before that, I had worked as a financial news writer for Reuters. Japan was known in the world then for its 'bubble' economy, and I felt as if I was working in a factory that assembled products called 'news'. I was dismayed with my career as a journalist and decided to study what journalism was. Looking back, I realised I was experiencing exactly the incipient stage of what Chapter 8 in *Power Without Responsibility* describes: the transformation of the press in the UK via concentration, commercialisation, polarisation and globalisation. The global phenomenon had also reached the corner of the East.

One of the first assignments given in graduate school was to read a chapter from *PWR*. Although it was used as a textbook—which usually deprives students of the joy of reading—this was truly enlightening because the book explained much of what I had experienced at Reuters and inspired me to reflect on the meaning of journalism more deeply. Of course, I never imagined at that time that I would have the honour of contributing a chapter in a collection whose main topic is that very book.

Slow to adapt to digitisation

Currently, journalism around the globe is undergoing a radical transformation led by technological innovation and social changes. But the traditional Japanese corporate media appear to be taking a different path or, at the very least, they have been adapting to this transformation only very slowly. On the surface, the Japanese media landscape seems to remain almost unchanged (McNeill and Hayashi 2022). The staid postwar constellation, dominated by five national mass newspapers as well as conventional terrestrial television networks, most of which are closely aligned with regional and national newspapers, remains very much alive. In addition, the close relationship between journalism and government officials, often characterised by cronyism, has remained the same as well.

One of the more recent cases of such cronyism happened in March 2020. As millions of Tokyoites were enduring the Covid-19 emergency measures, one of the nation's most powerful prosecutors, Hiromu Kurokawa, was caught mahjong gambling with two of his journalist friends from the right-wing *Sankei Shimbun* and from the liberal-left *Asahi Shimbun*. Kurokawa, the head of the Tokyo High Public Prosecutors Office, was at the time widely seen as Prime Minister Abe Shinzo's choice for Japan's top prosecutor and had already been in the news for months because he was able to remain in his post despite exceeding the conventional retirement age. He not only flaunted his disregard for lockdown rules, but he was also in breach of Japan's anti-gambling laws. But both newspapers—at opposite ends of Japan's political spectrum—explained very little to their millions of readers about what was discussed during the mahjong game.

Different types of vicious circle

As populism rises in the West, politics is becoming increasingly polarised and media distrust is growing. The vicious cycle of increased media polarisation and falling confidence in media appears to have accelerated. In the US, the so-called red and blue media penetrate political scenes and people's ways of life (Iyengar and Hahn 2009). Japan, by contrast, seems to be facing a different type of vicious circle.

Japanese postwar politics placed a strong emphasis on the development of its economic power. Politicians and bureaucrats prioritised the growth of large industries and companies over citizens' political involvement and personal wellbeing. Against this backdrop, Japanese people have developed little interest in political events. This has been evidenced in such cases as the low 56% voter turnout for the last Lower House election (the third lowest in the postwar period) or disinterest to share news with others

(Hayashi 2017). The vicious circle in Japan involves political disinterest, public apathy and indifference toward news and the media (Hayashi 2020).

With the spread of political apathy, the media are at the risk of becoming irrelevant. Japan's public broadcaster NHK surveyed people's intentions to participate in a variety of political actions, from signing a petition to writing an opinion letter to mass media. In this survey, a remarkable 76% of the respondents answered that they would never engage in writing letters to the media, highlighting the public's lack of interest and confidence in the media's ability to effect political changes. This trend is on the rise, even among the youth aged 16 to 29, a population segment typically considered more politically and idealistically inclined (Kobayashi 2015).

An ambivalent change

Amidst this depressing tendency, Japanese mainstream media are only slowly changing even with the proliferation of online media. This change, however, has brought about a mixed impact on Japanese society.

The Kurokawa gambling scandal mentioned above was first revealed by *Shūkan Bunshun*, a popular weekly magazine with a reputation for aggressive, confrontational reporting similar to that of British tabloids. Such weekly magazines, being 'latecomers' to the Japanese media market, have long been controversial in Japan's media landscape. For decades, they have sustained a mass-market (male) readership with its scandalism and sensationalism, exploiting the vacuum left by the insipid mainstream media. But it was one of these weekly magazines that showed the work of journalism, as it is supposed to work in liberal democracies, calling out abuses of power by government officials who might not otherwise feel the need to be accountable to the public (who pay their salaries as taxpayers).

Today, these 'guerilla'-like, second-class media have mostly gone online. People can purchase individual news items at affordable prices, and their impact is growing.

In particular, *Shūkan Bunshun* has become a symbol of the Japanese media's attempts to transform themselves as hyper-commercial, sensationalist, occasionally impertinent and irreverent. Manabu Shintani has been the man behind the aggressive publication. As the editor-in-chief, he advocated for cost-conscious management in an industry where, traditionally, the balance sheet had not been considered an important factor. In his book, he openly explains his 'business model' as follows:

> *Shūkan Bunshun* is steadily growing and differentiating itself from other media with its scoops. We intend to further promote digitization in the future to further enhance our power. In the *Shūkan Bunshun* editorial office, I developed a business model where we continue to produce a print weekly magazine while maximizing digital revenue through advertising and a subscription model, and branching out into books and merchandise. This strategy aims to sustain our organization's ability to produce scoops and investigative reports. (Shintani 2021, 86)

At the moment, it is not clear whether the nation-based system of 'static' journalism in Japan can survive amid sweeping net-driven liberalisation and globalisation.

Predicting whether Japanese journalism will become more or less 'free', or even 'better' in an age of digitisation is not easy either, because it is becoming increasingly difficult to clearly characterise 'Japanese media' as a homogeneous entity. It seems likely that we will see a further bifurcation of the Japanese media system: archaic, national-oriented media that are overly cautious and becoming irrelevant, and online media driven by a more personalised, extremely populistic and sensational approach. With these ever-polarising media worlds, Japanese society must find common ground to talk about the media's social responsibility, just as people do elsewhere in the world.

References

Curran, J. and Seaton J. 2018. *Power Without Responsibility: Press, Broadcasting and the Internet in Britain*, 8th edition. Routledge.

Hayashi, K. 2020. The Silent Public in a Liberal State: Challenges for Japan's Journalism in the Age of the Internet. In Y. Funabashi and G. J. Ikenberry (Eds.), *The Crisis of Liberal Internationalism: Japan and the World Order* (pp. 325–358). Brookings Institution Press.

Hayashi, K. 2017. Media Fushin: Naniga Towarete Irunoka ('Media Distrust. What is now at stake?') Iwanami-Shinsho (Japanese).

Iyengar, S. and Hahn, K. S. 2009. Red Media, Blue Media: Evidence of Ideological Selectivity in Media Use. *Journal of Communication*, 59, 19–39.

Kobayashi, T. 2015. Teikasuru Nihonjin no Seijiteki, Shakaiteki Katsudou Iyoku to Sono Haikei—ISSP Kokusai Hikaku Chōsa "Shimin Ishiki" Nihon no Kekka kara" *Hōso Kenkyu to Chōsa* January, 2015, NHK Hōso Bunka Kenkyu-jo. 22–41. ('The Declining Political and Social Activism of the Japanese and its Background: Results from the ISSP International Comparative Survey of Civic Consciousness, Japan.' *Japan Broadcasting Research and Survey.* NHK Broadcasting Culture Research Institute.) (Japanese)

McNeill, D. A. and Hayashi, K. 2022. Fringe Benefits: Weekly Magazines and Access Journalism in Japan. In S. Allan (Ed.), *The Routledge Companion to News and Journalism*, 2nd edition. Routledge.

Shintani, M. 2021. Toru Mamoru Kasegu Shūkan Bunshun 'Kikitoppa' Rīdaron ('Capture, Protect, Earn Shūkan Bunshun "Crisis Breakthrough" Leadership Theory'). Kōbunsha (Japanese).

CHAPTER 6

Reading *Power Without Responsibility* From the 'Periphery'

Vibodh Parthasarathi

Let me begin by recalling how I came across various editions of *PWR*. The earliest one reached me during the 1990s, courtesy of a photocopy from an associate who had returned from a summer fellowship in England. A subsequent edition was acquired by me about 15 years later for our then newly instituted departmental library. The most recent edition was sent to me as a PDF in the run-up to the workshop series organised by the Goldsmiths Leverhulme Media Research Centre in 2022. Such are the changing ways in which I, sitting in New Delhi, have come to access key works of occidental scholarship. This also indicates, more generally, how scholars in India tend to experience different regimes of circulation that have come to embody academic knowledge.

Reading *PWR* from the periphery is particularly fruitful given India's colonial encounter with Britain. Triggered by the few mentions of India in this book, three matters stood out for me.

One was about porting ideas of press governance from the heart of the colonial empire to the hinterlands of India. As in Britain, newspaper publishers in 19th-century India were mandated to pay a deposit to the government, making them vulnerable to the regimes of the day. But we also note the inability, or disinterest, to transplant other regulatory mechanisms from Britain—such as stamp duty, extensively examined in *PWR*. The array of ideas ported to India suggests that colonial governance adopted the most crude and direct measures to treat newspapers exclusively as a political force, rather than (additionally) as an economic activity (see Sonwalkar 2015, Kalpagam 2002). This lack of regulating the press indirectly through economic measures imparted significant path dependencies in the history of press policy in postcolonial India.

We also see, secondly, the distortion of institutional initiatives after travelling to India; a prime example is public broadcasting, about which *PWR* mounts a passionate but critical defence. Circumstances distorting public broadcasting across postcolonial India, Bangladesh, Pakistan and Sri Lanka, have been well documented (for instance, Pendakur 1989, Rahman 2014, Sulehria 2017, Weerasinghe 2023). But across South Asia, the appeal of public broadcasting, as argued by Curran and Seaton amongst others, is impeded by another factor. I find the normative and ideological underpinnings of such arguments take for granted a certain kind of state which is at odds with what we have learnt about the nature of the state and state formation in South Asia.

Notwithstanding these insertions and distortions, thirdly, I observe a key commonality in the dynamics of press development across Britain and India. This is clearly palpable if we follow *PWR*'s insistence of examining the press, and by extension all news media, as a constellation of interests. In both settings, a set of dominant interests in the news media have impeded incubating a certain kind of press and certain values within the press. Furthermore, these interests constituting the press have recurrently stonewalled calls for public accountability and scrutiny.

All this leads me to point at two of the most significant methodological contributions of *PWR*. One is that it comprehensively demonstrates that media history and media policy are not separate intellectual pursuits. This is contra to how these 'sub-fields' of media studies are typically configured in curricula, taught in classrooms, pursued by scholars and curated in conferences. The other is about the book's imagination of the news media not being scarred by compartmentalised studies of print, broadcasting and the internet. This expanded imagination, interrelating ideas, interests and institutions across all sites of the news media, is precisely what enables *PWR* to straddle a vast temporal canvas—something reflected in its changing subtitle from the first to the later editions.

Yet, a seminal contribution like *PWR* is not as popular in India as it should be. In fact, its approach and canvas are at odds with the dominant trends in teaching and research I see around me. Let me try to reason out, perhaps even to speculate about, this claim.

Foremost, the study of the media in all its material forms in India has traditionally been reduced to the study of news content; at best, it has relied primarily on the analysis of reportage. Secondly, I see a presentist, largely event-oriented, approach dotting scholarship on the news media. A large share of South Asian scholarship, both in situ and diasporic, gets triggered and confined by happenings, mis-happenings, and related personalities marking our times. Consequently, *PWR* has limited appeal amidst the methodological normalisation of content analysis and presentism in the study of the news media in and on India.

Thirdly, there is a medium-centric approach dominating scholarship on news in India. Newspapers, broadcast news and online journalism have been imagined as distinct, sometimes even autonomous fields. Interestingly, these three sites of the media have become associated with different phases of independent India's political economy. The substantive expansion of newspapers began in the early 1980s when the values of nation-building still dominated media policy; private broadcast news emerged out of incremental deregulation commenced during the 1990s; and digital news outlets mushroomed in the wake of neoliberal transnationalisation over the past decade. In other words, these three renditions of the news media are associated with two significant shifts in India's political economy. In fact, the celebration of these shifts, and accompanying ruptures, are a key theme in scholarship on broadcast news and online journalism—something I would be very cautious to do. What we need is a handle that can straddle these three renditions of the press, their materialities, and the temporalities they constitute—something which successive editions of *PWR* have achieved.

The presentist, content-centric, and medium-centric orientation of scholarship on and from India may have something to do with the fourth factor whittling the appeal of *PWR*—the absence of, and the lack of interest to develop, a robust body of work on the histories of the news media. There are two reasons for this absence, one holding true across South Asian scholarship while the other is peculiar to India. Media studies in South Asia started coming into its own from the late 1990s; consequently, it 'leapfrogged' to examine the then emergent milieu of satellite broadcasting and subsequently that around the internet. So the formative conditions within which the print press emerged in India, dating back to the 19th century, have remained grossly underexplored. Numerous antiquarian or 'corporate' accounts of press and television history have, rather unfortunately, become the staple for undergraduate and graduate students in India.

Moreover, accounts of the news media (including their past) have been enslaved by a certain methodological regionalism in India. This goes back to press development, and until recently press culture, having evolved differently within India's numerous linguistic geographies—which over time have come to embody India's different linguistic media markets. These vastly distinct linguistic geographies make it difficult for any comprehensive 'national' history, especially of the sort articulated by Curran and Seaton. Equally, it makes it difficult to teach comparative regional histories; particularly if we remain wedded to the study of news content, which involves multi-lingual proficiencies, not just in making sense of print and broadcast news but also of numerous archives across the country.

Amidst the absence of robust media histories, how do we see the particular project of media policy history—of which *PWR* is an enduring exemplifier? Here, I would like to reiterate the congenital traction between the pursuits of media history, journalism studies and media policy; they cannot, and should not be seen as pulling students of the media in opposite directions. There is a pressing need for journalism studies in India to involve historical and institutional questions; in the same vein, I would urge my colleagues in media policy studies to historicise their imagination and canvas. This is something I have been attempting in my ongoing work on Indian media policy in the *moyenne durée* (see Parthasarathi 2021). One of the longstanding tensions I have been trying to engage with is that between freedom of the press, and freedom in the press. *PWR* of course joins hands with other equally extensive efforts to engage with this tension, Edwin Baker being one of the prime exponents.

This then takes me to the last reason for *PWR* not being as popular in India as it deserves: that of the geopolitics of academic knowledge. This speaks to the overarching influence of US scholarship in media studies across India. Of course, the prime reasons for this are the large number of diasporic Indian scholars across the Atlantic, given the sheer scale of the academic-industrial complex in the USA. This leads to debates of how a periphery engages with the centres of academic power in our times, something which deserves an altogether different set of reflections from across the world.

References

Baker, C. Edwin. 2004. *Media, Markets, and Democracy*. Cambridge University Press, New York.

Kalpagam, U. 2002. Colonial Governmentality and the Public Sphere in India. *Journal of Historical Sociology*, 15(1), 35–58.

Parthasarathi, V. 2021. Dismembering Media Diversity: A Tryst with Two Press Commissions. *Media, Culture & Society*, 43(4), 764–775.

Pendakur, M. 1989. Indian Television Comes of Age: Liberalization and the Rise of Consumer Culture. *Communication*, 11(1), 177–197.

Rahman, A. 2014. The Problems with Reimagining Public Media in the Context of Global South. *Stream: Culture/Politics/Technology*, 6(1), 56–65. http://journals.sfu.ca/cpt/index.php/stream/index

Sonwalkar, P. 2015. Indian Journalism in the Colonial Crucible. *Journalism Studies*, 16(5), 624–636.

Sulehria, F. 2017. DD and PTV as Victims of Media Globalisation. *Asian Journal of Communication*, 27(1), 97–112.

Weerasinghe, P.N. 2023. From State to Public Service: Legal and Structural Constraints in the Sri Lankan Broadcasting Sphere. *International Journal of Media and Communication Research*, 4(2), 1–16. https://journal.uir.ac.id/index.php/ijmcr/article/view/12907/5464

CHAPTER 7

Big Tech's Influx into Africa:
A Case of *Power Without Responsibility*

Winston Mano and L. Lusike Mukhongo

Introduction

Africa has become a magnet for big tech companies, arguably for self-serving and speculative business explorations aimed at dominating global digital ecologies. Companies such as Meta, Amazon, Apple, Netflix, Google, Microsoft and Orange are involved in a fierce competitive takeover of Africa's digital ecosystem. Evidence from Africa shows that big tech's conduct is extractive, anti-competitive and profit-oriented, and undermines and exploits local talent, interests and initiatives (Mano 2022). Contrary to the assertion that new technology equals progress, the primary objective of big tech companies coming to Africa has been to mine data in ways that reproduce colonial logics (Benyera 2021; Mano 2022).

The arrival of big tech platforms is amounting to a new form of absolute colonial power, depriving Africans of their digital dividends. Narratives tend to project positive portrayals while hiding the ugly side of the impact of big tech interventions. The behaviour of big techs contradicts the expectation that those with immense power ought to refrain from inflicting pain on others, according to an Ethiopian proverb. There is a growing need for myth-busting accounts to name and shame big tech's transgressions in Africa to protect public interest in communications. It is urgent and imperative to examine the ramifications of this growing interest and to relate it to debates in our field, including UNESCO benchmarks for new technologies (MacBride 1980; UNESCO 2023).

This chapter critiques the role of these global tech corporations in Africa in the light of evidence showing that they constitute a new form of 'power without responsibility' that is detrimental to the public interest of Africans in the communications area (Willems 2016; Nothias 2020). This account of big tech in Africa resonates with the 'irresponsible' behaviour of press barons discussed by Curran and Seaton in *Power Without Responsibility*, sponsoring new forms of interference and policy issues. The chapter offers initial but important pointers as to what can be characterised irresponsible conduct by the big tech companies.

The influx of big tech in Africa

The emerging forms of transnational digital communication monopolies are rooted in monopoly global capitalism, a direct beneficiary of an emerging global liberal market framework that promotes the idea that the 'profitability of media businesses would be enhanced through relaxation of ownership rules' (Freedman 2008, 178). From a neoliberal perspective, policymakers argue against strong regulations and ownership rules for communications. Despite a growing population of commercially lucrative internet users in Africa, there are 'fewer laws or no laws guiding digital media. This leaves the continent's population and economies unprotected and at the mercy of big techs from Silicon Valley' (Nwankwo 2019).

Apart from a weak regulatory framework, Mano (2022) adds that the two other forces drawing big tech companies to Africa are, on the one hand, technological innovation, natural resources, rapid urbanisation and a youthful population, and on the other, a vast pool of African consumers, digitally savvy and connected locally and globally by mobile technologies. African countries in search of development put more emphasis on tech interventions, and this was the case with Kenya, commonly referred to as the 'Silicon Savannah', where in 2006, with a 'vision for a prosperous ICT-driven Kenyan society', the National Information Communication Technology Policy was launched to promote internet access to urban and rural areas (National ICT Policy 2006, 1). As Mukhongo (2020) argues, on the back of neoliberal frameworks, Africa shows a keen desire to position itself as the central technology hub, with countries such as Kenya emerging as regional technology hubs. China's Alibaba also extended its international trading platform to Rwanda (2018) and Ethiopia (2019) as both countries sought to leverage their digital commerce. However, there is a need to unpack the growing relationships between international and local actors when 'implementing new technologies' in Africa (Garliardone 2016). The problem is that big tech companies are often naively received without criticality, and often as saviours within development-starved African contexts.

The growing power of big tech in Africa relates to its 'ability to prevent the actions of other groups and individuals' (Naím 2013, 16). As Michalis (2021) argues, power is at the centre of communication policy, and whether visible, invisible or structural, it remains relevant to all aspects of policymaking. In this context, policy actors exhibit diverse and occasionally divergent objectives, with big tech companies seeking profits and expanded market control, juxtaposed with African states aiming for developmental applications of technology. The policy objectives of big tech, therefore, have clashed with those of African states, underscoring the urgency to reconcile these disparities before they exacerbate further. The problem manifests in a new form of digital colonialism, also referred to as data colonialism.

Data colonialism

Digital colonialism denotes a contemporary Scramble for Africa, envisioned as a Scramble for Data as big tech companies compete to extract, process and control user data for financial gain and market dominance while offering minimum benefits to the communities that the data is extracted from. The coveted asset or 'new gold' in the scramble for Africa's digital future is the vast population of newly accessible (mobile phone) African consumers, made possible by continuous digital connectivity that intertwines with local and global products and services.

Kwet (2022) points out that private ownership of crucial physical infrastructure like 'cloud-server farms, wireless mobile networks, and transoceanic submarine cables' primarily benefits the owners with, for example, Amazon and Microsoft expanding their cloud centres globally, embedding costly machinery alongside proprietary software and intensifying reliance on their products. In his book, Benyera (2021) observes that big tech companies already own and control massive amounts of big data, artificial intelligence, online communities and the online economy but are keen to take advantage of Africa to enhance their data interests.

The involvement of big tech in Africa underscores an extractive dynamic, perpetuating data colonialism. The current power dynamics surrounding data ownership and control imbalances necessitate a critical research agenda involving designing and implementing relational accountability frameworks prioritising African stakeholders (Mano 2022). To emphasise the extractive logic at work, Benyera (2021, ix) rightly observes that 'Like other forms of capital, data extraction is not only unethical but also brutal and unforgiving. Data is capital and perceived as the contemporary equivalent of gold and oil; it has power and, like all forms of power, it is strategically deployed within political spaces to predetermine, influence, and pre-empt political decisions'. Kwet (2019) similarly critiques digital colonialism as structural domination through centralised ownership and control of the 'digital ecosystem's core pillars (software, hardware, and network connectivity)' that foster the consolidation of political, economic and social power in the hands of 'GAFAM' (Google/Alphabet, Amazon, Facebook, Apple and Microsoft) along with state intelligence agencies emerging as modernday imperialists on the global stage. There are also lingering questions about how Facebook's Free Basics project, banned in India following nationwide protests about net neutrality, has expanded without much public scrutiny to some 32 countries (Nothias 2020, 329). Of equal concern is the observation by Garliardone (2016, n.p.) that 'the Italian company Hacking Team was contracted to target Ethiopian journalists and opposition leaders in the diaspora, using spyware to access their files, passwords, and intercept their communications'. He adds that 'FinSpy, a commercial software developed by UK- and Germany-based Gamma International, was purchased to perform similar operations' (ibid.). The role of American intelligence in training Ethiopian spies was also evident from files released by Edward Snowden. It is, therefore, worrying that big techs are implicated in stifling activism and alternative politics through the profitable business of selling surveillance technologies to authoritarian leaders in Africa. Mano (2022) supports efforts to dig deeper into these issues, contending that, if left alone, big tech companies will continue to compete for control over Africa's digital ecosystem using unethical and discredited means.

Africa as a sales office

Big tech companies are conveniently characterising Africa as an 'insignificant region' within the global digital ecology; a move that allows them to establish 'sales and support offices' rather than (much more needed) 'knowledge development centres' (Manaileng 2021). Africa needs innovation hubs and tech infrastructure rather than sales offices. For example, X set up such an office in Ghana in 2022, employing only 11 Ghanaians. This followed the establishment of Google's artificial intelligence lab in Ghana in 2019 which was again not a full collaboration with locals, while Amazon and Meta have also opened marketing and sales offices in Johannesburg, South Africa.

The above-mentioned examples show that big tech companies are exploitatively leveraging Africa to stay ahead of their rivals by dominating and controlling Africa's emerging digital market under the guise of investments, collaborations and partnerships. In an interview, Manaileng, a South African data scientist, argues that 'when the tech giants come to Africa, they must come to provide knowledge development and not just enhancing their attempt to sell their products' (quoted in Yeo 2021). Africans, Manaileng argues, could enter the market if they 'own innovations rather than follow the trends and sell the products of other countries' (ibid.). It is critical that we have African talent at the centre of the technology sector. Big tech platforms in Africa are also implicated in disinformation campaigns ranging from state-sponsored propaganda using click armies and troll farms to silence opposition voices to data analytics firms such as Cambridge Analytica selling insidious toolkits to politicians in elections in Kenya and Nigeria (Ndlela and Mano 2018; Grohmann and Corpus 2024). The dissemination of such falsehoods erodes public trust and undermines the process of democratisation in the global South.

The Kenyan case of labour (in)visibilities

Big tech also makes labour invisible, particularly for people of colour and from the global South. Meta and other tech companies have been outsourcing content moderation work to the global South through extractive and exploitative labour practices, paying workers abysmal wages, often less than $2 per hour, and subjecting them to psychological trauma and denying their unionising rights. Content moderators in Kenya have raised concerns about the huge psychological toll on workers when they are confronted with traumatising graphic content (Hendrix 2023; Perrigo 2022). A former content moderator for Meta filed a lawsuit claiming that the substandard working conditions faced by contracted content moderators violated the Kenyan constitution and further argued that the content moderators in Kenya were subjected to unacceptable working conditions, irregular pay, insufficient mental health support and union suppression tactics (Mersie 2022).

In 2024, a Kenyan content moderator for OpenAI filed a petition for the Kenyan government to conduct a comprehensive inquiry into the working conditions of contractors responsible for reviewing and moderating content generated by OpenAI's ChatGPT. In 2023, 184 moderators in Kenya sued Meta and two contractors, arguing their union organising efforts had cost them their jobs. There were also serious allegations of third-party contractor abuses, including worker exploitation and unfair termination. They also accused Meta of failing to stop hate speech. When ChatGPT was released to the public in 2022, it was lauded as a groundbreaking technological innovation due to its ability to generate text content for varied contexts and uses (Zaitsu and Jin 2023). ChatGPT, however, outsourced content moderators from Kenya to work on making their AI less toxic while the Kenyan workers who worked on it were paid a meagre salary of $2 per hour. Another case of labour precarity was revealed by CNN in July 2023 in relation to cost-cutting Twitter layoffs and the differentials in how employees based in Africa were treated as opposed to those in other locations. The former employees of Twitter Africa, based in Accra, had reportedly not received their severance pay or further communication from the company for more than seven months since being laid off.

From the cases discussed above, it is evident that the big tech scramble in Africa is also deeply intertwined with the crisis of global capitalism, over-accumulation (Harris 2019) and labour precarity. It contributes to the emergence of a social underclass facing precarious employment, lack of job security and unstable incomes.

Conclusion

The increasing concentration of market power within the technology sector mirrors the broader trends of wealth and corporate power centralisation prevalent in the neoliberal era, fostering unrestrained expansion and extractive practices by big tech companies in Africa and the global South. Mano (2022) points out that while big tech companies can be harbingers of technology and capital transfer to Africa and other developing nations, it is also essential to focus on the exploitative logics they perpetuate in Africa and the global South. The recent surge of big tech into Africa highlights its pursuit of investment opportunities in emerging markets and raises questions about 'digital colonialism' and the exacerbation of media and cultural imperialism due to inequities in North-South information and technology flows. Humanising digital ecologies in the public interest is urgent and imperative for all rather than projecting Africans as digital subjects. From an Afrokological perspective, this chapter foregrounds a new relational accountability between big techs and locals (Mano and Milton 2021). It is an attempt to restrain and push back on big tech's power without responsibility and is an urgent call for African interests to be placed at the centre of digital policy frameworks.

References

Benyera, E. 2021. *The Fourth Industrial Revolution and the Recolonisation of Africa*. Routledge.

Freedman, D. 2008. *The Politics of Media Policy*. Polity.

Gagliardone, I. 2021. Chinese Digital Tech in Africa: Moral Panics and the Messy Reality of Surveillance. LSE published 20 May 2021: https://shorturl.at/uxO27 (accessed 1 February 2024).

Grohmann, R. and Corpus Ong, J. 2024. Disinformation-for-Hire as Everyday Digital Labor: Introduction to the Special Issue. *Social Media + Society*, 10(1). https://doi.org/10.1177/20563051231224723 (accessed 31 January 2024).

Harris, J. 2019. The Future of Globalization: Neo-Fascism or the Green New Deal. *Race & Class*, 61(1), 3–25. https://doi.org/10.1177/0306396819844121 (accessed 31 January 2024).

Hendrix, J. 2023. Checking on the Progress of Content Moderators in Africa. https://www.techpolicy.press/checking-on-the-progress-of-content-moderators-in-africa/ (accessed 31 January 2024).

Kwet, M. 2019. Digital Colonialism: US Empire and the New Imperialism in the Global South. *Race & Class*, 60(4), 3–26. https://doi.org/10.1177/030639681 8823172 (accessed 21 January 2024).

Kwet, M. 2022. The Digital Tech Deal: A Socialist Framework for the Twenty-First Century. *Race & Class*, 63(3), 63–84. https://doi-org.libproxy.library.wmich.edu/10.1177/03063968211064478 (accessed 22 January 2024).

MacBride, S. 1980. *Many Voices, One World: Towards a New, More Just and More Efficient World Information and Communication Order*. International Commission for the Study of Communication Problems report. UNESCO.

Manaileng, M. 2021. On the Deplorable Relationship of South Africa and Big Tech Companies. *LinkedIn*, April 13, available at: https://www.linkedin.com/pulse/deplorable-relationship-south-africa-big-tech-mabu-manaileng/ (accessed 31 January 2024).

Mano, W. 2022. Big Tech's Scramble for Africa. In W. Mano and L. El Mkaouar (Eds.), *Media Ownership in Africa in the Digital Age* (pp. 15–31). Routledge.

Mano, W. and Milton, V. (Eds.) 2021. *The Routledge Handbook of African Media and Communication Studies*. Routledge.

Mersie, A. 2022. Content Moderator in Kenya Sues Facebook-owner Meta Over Working Conditions. *Insurance Journal*, 10 May. Available at: https://www.insurancejournal.com/news/international/2022/05/10/667021.htm (accessed 21 January 2024).

Michalis, M. 2021. Why Should We Care About Media Policy? Critical Directions in Media Policy Research. In P. McDonald (Ed.), *The Routledge Companion to Media Industries* (pp. 66–75). Routledge.

Ministry of Information and Communications. 2006. National Information and Communications Technology ICT Policy. https://www.researchictafrica.net/countries/kenya/National_ICT_Policy_2006.pdf (accessed 30 January 2024).

Mukhongo, L. L. 2020. Participatory Media Cultures: Virality, Humour, and Online Political Contestations in Kenya. *Africa Spectrum*, 55(2), 148–169. https://doi.org/10.1177/0002039720957014 (accessed 21 January 2024).

Naím, E. 2013. *The End of Power: From Boardrooms to Battlefields and Churches to States, Why Being in Charge isn't What it Used to be*. Basic Books.

Ndlela, M. N. and Mano, W. 2020. The Changing Face of Election Campaigning in Africa. In M. Ndlela and W. Mano (Eds.) *Social Media and Elections in Africa*, Volume 1 (pp. 1–12). Palgrave Macmillan.

Nothias, T. 2020. Access Granted: Facebook's Free Basics in Africa. *Media, Culture and Society*, 42(3), 329–348. https://doi.org/10.1177/0163443719890530 (accessed 30 January 2024).

Nwankwo E. J. 2019. African Tech for African Problems. *The Republic*, 3(13), available at https://republic.com.ng/vol3-no3/african-tech-for-african-problems/ (accessed 21 January 2024).

Perrigo, B. 2022. Inside Facebook's African Sweatshop. *Time Magazine*, 199(7), 32.

UNESCO 2023. *Guidelines for the Governance of Digital Platforms: Safeguarding Freedom of Expression and Access to Information Through a Multi-Stakeholder Approach*. UNESCO [7111] ISBN: 978-92-3-100620-3. Available: https://unesdoc.unesco.org/ark:/48223/pf0000387339 (accessed 01 February 2023).

Willems, W. 2016. Beyond Free Basics: Facebook, Data Bundles and Zambia's Social Media Internet. https://blogs.lse.ac.uk/africaatlse/2016/09/01/beyond-free-basics-facebook-data-bundles-and-zambias-social-media-internet/ (accessed 31 January 2024).

Yeo, H. 2021. Mabu Manaileng: Setting Trends with AI and ML in Africa with Datawizzards. *Medium*, 12 May, available at: https://medium.com/atoti/mabu-manaileng-setting-trends-with-ai-and-ml-in-africa-with-datawizzards-f6ef589d67d0 (accessed 21 January 2024).

Zaitsu, W. and Jin, M. 2023. Distinguishing ChatGPT. *PloS One*, 18(8), e0288453. https://doi.org/10.1371/journal.pone.0288453 (accessed 31 January 2024).

CHAPTER 8

Power, Money and Arab Media: A Not-so-simple Saga

Naomi Sakr

As the authors of *Power Without Responsibility* acknowledge in summarising media developments in a region they call the Middle East, 'the story is never simple' (Curran and Seaton 2018, 434). Their comment is prompted by seemingly contradictory trends: on one hand, the content available to local populations is increasing and diversifying and on the other, threats to journalists and media initiatives are intensifying—all against a background of the potentially 'catastrophic' cost of ignorance and a loss of knowledge (Curran and Seaton 2018, 442). Far from being the truism it might have been, the implicit warning against simplification is relevant to much that has been written about Arab media over several decades and is one that has been issued periodically by specialist scholars (e.g. Tawil-Souri 2008, 1407–09; Sakr 2012 and 2016; Iskandar 2014, 252). The present short essay explores some of the reservations expressed, with the aim of highlighting how they have been, and can be, overcome.

It may be no wonder that, since so much commentary on Arab media has been published outside the region in languages other than Arabic, concerns have been raised about the dominance of Western perspectives and a lack of attention paid to diversity in and between countries in the region. Those concerns are not solely attributed to what one critic has called a 'superiority complex' within 'Western government circles' (Tawil-Souri 2008, 1408). A 2016 review of eight decades of communication studies in the Arab world, written by a US-educated former presenter with Jordanian TV who has held senior academic positions in the United Arab Emirates since the 1990s, concluded that the field evolved locally in the 'shadows of Western-centric intellectual traditions', being constrained in the intellectual contributions it could make to global communication studies by factors such as 'limited freedom of speech' in Arab institutions and a 'lack of collaboration among Arab scholars' (Ayish 2016, 489). A French-educated Tunisian professor of media, who served briefly on his country's post-uprising audiovisual regulatory body before resigning in protest at its undemocratic workings in 2015 (Klaus 2023, 71–72), made a similar observation in an essay on the possibility of pursuing cultural studies in Arab higher education. Noting that the proliferation of satellite channels and the so-called digital revolution had sparked an uncritical renewal of developmentalist theses aligned with those of Lerner, Schramm and others, Riadh Ferjani (2012, 106, 115–116) observed that 'rare pieces' of research[1] linking 'macro and micro perspectives, structural analysis and thick description, critical political economy and cultural studies' were conducted 'outside Arab universities,' apparently 'forced into exile' because of their failure to 'legitimate the [local] social order and its violence.'

These analyses tend to undermine any implication that an analysis of Arab media can be readily characterised on the basis of its author's background, mother tongue, employment or even scholarly discipline. Arab writers employed by research institutions in the US or UK have been criticised for exhibiting the same faults they attribute to their Western-born counterparts. A review of Mamoun Fandy's 2007 book *(Un)Civil War of Words*, about the relationship between Arab politics and media, argued that Fandy could 'not escape certain Western biases, the very ones he criticises' and found that his 'sweeping generalisations' could 'lead to misunderstandings' in failing to acknowledge different political cultures across different Arab states and adopting a 'monolithic understanding of censorship' (Archibald and Guidère 2008, 994–95, 997). Fouad Ajami's diatribe against Al-Jazeera, published under the title 'What the Muslim world is watching' in the *New York Times Magazine* in November 2001, soon after the 9/11 suicide attacks, prompted a US translator of Arabic to describe him as a 'bitter intellectual… cynically exploiting his exotic appeal to the media by pandering to the prejudices of the society that has granted him his privileged perch' (Wilmsen 2002).

In light of concerns about a failure to say anything 'interesting' on the 'plurality of real tendencies among Arabs of diverse backgrounds and experiences' or to connect 'shifts in media' to 'real shifts on the ground' (Tawil-Souri 2008, 1408), it should be noted that much English-language writing on Arab media before the 2000s was country-specific and interdisciplinary. William Rugh's *The Arab Press: News Media and Political Process in the Arab World*, published in 1979, offered a questionable typology based on data from individual countries and their diverse media systems. Douglas Boyd's *Broadcasting in the Arab World*, first released in 1982 and updated in 1993 and 1999, presented a country-by-country, sector-by-sector, descriptive account of production and distribution decisions made in the early days of radio and television in the region. Nabil Dajani's study, *Disoriented Media in a Fragmented Society: The Lebanese Experience*, published by the American University of Beirut in 1982 during the Lebanese civil war, covered Lebanese history, politics and society. When Walter Armbrust's edited collection, *Mass Mediations: New Approaches to Popular Culture in the Middle East and Beyond*, came out in 2000, developed from conference papers delivered in the mid-1990s, it was testimony to years of research already carried out by anthropologists like Armbrust in Egypt and Christa Salamandra in Syria. It demonstrated a belief that mass-mediated art and entertainment, with all that implies in terms of economics, politics and nation-state frameworks, can 'never be understood in isolation,' being a form that 'mediates the homogenizing tendencies of global culture' on a national scale (Armbrust 2000, 26).

An urge to shift from the national to trying to understand the Arabic-speaking region as a whole was arguably a natural outcome of the rise of pan-Arab satellite broadcasting during the 1990s. The political, technological and economic factors behind this development in regionwide television caused a proliferation of channels in the 2000s (Sakr 2001, 2007, 2023) and, with it, an unprecedented burst of scholarly attention accompanied by an upsurge in activity by a wide range of international funding and human rights monitoring bodies as well as the marketing and advertising trade press. This in turn generated a step-change in the type and volume of data available for serious political-economic scrutiny of the field, as personal insights from practitioners and policy makers emerged at workshops and roundtables in Arab cities, alongside facts and figures recorded in reports compiled by non-governmental organisations based inside and outside the region. The founding of *Transnational Broadcasting Studies* at the American University in Cairo in 1998 provided a novel venue for a range of writing and research about all aspects of the region's media; its renaming as *Arab Media & Society* in 2007 came in response to rapid change in the media landscape, as did the launch of the *Middle East Journal of Culture and Communication* in 2008.

The 2000s also saw a new generation of researchers from Arab countries graduate with PhDs from universities in Europe and North America, just as people everywhere were taking up the opportunities of digital technology and social media to communicate in new ways, through blogging, then video sharing, then live-streaming and much more. Two decades on, the names of members of that generation adorn the voluminous 'handbooks' and 'companions' that publishers have taken to producing on Arab communication and culture. Keen to discard discredited developmentalist models and essentialist assumptions, their varied approaches and interest in critical theory vastly enriched insights into the political economy of Arab media. Tellingly, the sixth and last seminar in an international series on the topic hosted by the Communication and Media Research Institute at the University of Westminster between 2003 and 2005 bore the title 'Arab Public Sphere: A Convenient Illusion?' They were not able, however, to shift Western perceptions ahead of the Arab uprisings of 2010–11 in a way that would pre-empt misplaced neoliberal expectations about the disruption of state activity opening up media markets and making way for competing private sector alternatives. As James Curran had observed in 2004, the role of markets in the functioning of the media is not predetermined. Citing Sakr (2001), he contrasted the 'highly politicized and state-penetrated market' limiting media autonomy in Arab states with suggestions made elsewhere that the 'market exerts an emancipatory influence on the media in the context of authoritarian societies' (Curran 2004, 25).

The uprisings were not able to end close relations between media owners and former regime incumbents, resolve long-entrenched distortions in the advertising market or unpick multiple layers of official control imposed nationally and regionally through media laws, penal codes and informal agreements among those who stood to lose out from changes in the status quo. For these features of the media scene to be disrupted on sufficient scale would have required foresight and commitment on the part of US and European governments and policy makers far beyond the sectoral support provided by a myriad of media development agencies. It needed wholesale upheaval of a kind not consistent with Western leaders' fears about who would replace the Arab dictators they relied on to contain Islamism and not consistent with Western onlookers' favoured 'transition paradigm,' which blithely assumes 'political history, institutional legacies… sociocultural traditions, or other "structural" features' will not be 'major factors' in where the putative transition leads (Carothers 2002, 8). Arab media arrangements, like other structural features of these countries' authoritarian political systems, have been and remain subject to 'limited access orders' whereby political elites ensure their survival through patronage and clientelism, following an Ottoman tradition that was 'reinforced by colonial powers before becoming incorporated into post-colonial states,' in which access to public goods and services is handed out in return for political support (Springborg 2020, 62–64).

If anything, this feature of the political economy of Arab media has deepened since 2011 and there must be doubts about scholars' ability to track its outcomes closely in the 2020s because of the way censorship and surveillance intensify as authoritarianism in some countries turns into totalitarianism. Since the military takeover in Egypt in 2013 and the mass killings of protestors by government forces a few weeks later, Egyptian media ownership has been centralised under state organs (Guaaybess 2021, 417–420), draconian curbs have been imposed on civil society access to external assistance and blocks placed on information websites. In 2016, Cambridge University doctoral candidate Guilio Regeni was abducted, tortured and murdered in Egypt while studying the country's labour unions. Meanwhile global tech giants' complicity with controls in Egypt (Abdulla 2021, 430–431) and across the region (Sakr 2022, 48–52) added a further dimension to what was being termed 'digital authoritarianism'. In war-torn Syria, Silicon Valley-based platforms became the 'de facto gatekeepers' of the country's post-2011 visual history, responsible for 'removing a dramatic amount of Syrian-generated content without notice' and thereby revealing the 'fragility of the digital commons, originated as a collective practice, later expropriated and appropriated by the very few' (Della Ratta 2018, 173, 177). Marc Owen Jones (2022, 13) lays out the case for regarding Saudi Arabia as a 'new digital superpower, at least in the realms of deception via social media, specifically Twitter,' able to 'launch influence operations on three fronts—domestically, regionally and internationally—in a sustained and evolving manner.'

Today, research into the effects of ownership and control on what gets left out of Arab media content is as important as it ever was, if not more so. In his last column for *The Washington Post*, published posthumously after his brutal murder at the Saudi Arabian consulate in Istanbul in October 2018, Saudi journalist Jamal Khashoggi lamented the lack of uncensored platforms for Arab voices. Citing findings from the latest Freedom House *Freedom in the World* report, he argued that a public that is either uninformed or misinformed is 'unable to adequately address, much less publicly discuss, matters that affect the region and their day-to-day lives' (Khashoggi 2018). At that point Tunisia was identified as the only Arab country where the press could be classified as 'free'. Since then, even that glimmer has been extinguished, as the president elected in 2019 on a promise of standing up to a corrupt elite set about dismantling Tunisia's hard-won democratic institutions. That Tunisia was nonetheless awarded €1bn of EU money in July 2023 reflects a pattern of western governments' 'nonchalance towards authoritarianism' (Gani 2022, 65), evident in Arab countries since colonial and postcolonial times and particularly striking in the face of clampdowns on civil and political rights since the mid-2010s. To avoid oversimplifying the political economy of Arab media, probing foreign involvement is one place to start.

Note

1   Ferjani's example (2012, 115) is Lila Abu-Lughod's 2005 ethnographic study of the production and reception of Egyptian TV serials, *Dramas of Nationhood*. Abu-Lughod is Professor of Anthropology at Columbia University.

References

Abdulla, R. 2021. Tweeting the Revolution: The Evolution of Social Media Use in Egypt's Turbulent Times. In R. Springborg et al. (Eds.) *The Routledge Handbook on Contemporary Egypt* (pp. 422–434). Routledge.

Archibald, J. and Guidère, M. 2008. Understanding the Media's Language of War. *Middle Eastern Studies*, 44(6), 993–1007.

Armbrust, W. 2000. Introduction: Anxieties of Scale. In W. Armbrust (Ed.), *Mass Mediations: New Approaches to Popular Culture in the Middle East and Beyond* (pp. 1–31). University of California Press.

Ayish, M. I. 2016. Communication Studies in the Arab World. In P. Simonson and D. W. Park (Eds.), *The International History of Communication Study* (pp. 474–493). Routledge.

Boyd, D. A. (1999) *Broadcasting in the Arab World: A Survey of the Electronic Media in the Middle East*, 3rd edition. Iowa State University Press.

Carothers, T. 2002. The End of the Transition Paradigm. *Journal of Democracy*, 13(1), 5–21.

Curran, J. 2004. The Rise of the Westminster School. In A. Calabrese and C. Sparks (Eds.), *Toward a Political Economy of Culture: Capitalism and Communication in the Twenty-First Century* (pp. 13–40). Rowman & Littlefield.

Curran, J. and Seaton, J. (2018) *Power Without Responsibility: Press, Broadcasting and the Internet in Britain*, 8th edition. Routledge.

Dajani, N. H. (1992) *Disoriented Media in a Fragmented Society: The Lebanese Experience*. American University of Beirut.

Della Ratta, D. 2018. *Shooting a Revolution: Visual Media and Warfare in Syria*. Pluto Press.

Ferjani, R. 2012. In Search of the Great Absence: Cultural Studies in Arab Universities In T. Sabry (Ed.), *Arab Cultural Studies: Mapping the Field* (pp. 101–122). I B Tauris.

Gani, J. K. 2022. From Discourse to Practice: Orientalism, Western Policy and the Arab Uprisings. *International Affairs*, 98(1), 45–65.

Guaaybess, T. 2021. Media ownership in Egypt (2000–2020): Categories and Configurations. In R. Springborg et al. (Eds.), *The Routledge Handbook on Contemporary Egypt* (pp. 412–423). Routledge.

Iskandar, A. 2014. Defying Definition: Toward Reflexivity in 'Arab media' Studies. In L. Hudson, A. Iskandar and M. Kirk (Eds.), *Media Evolution on the Eve of the Arab Spring* (pp. 251–265). Palgrave Macmillan.

Jones, M. O. 2022. *Digital Authoritarianism in the Middle East: Deception, Disinformation and Social Media*. Oxford University Press.

Khashoggi, J. 2018. What the Arab World Needs Most is Free Expression. *The Washington Post*, 17 October.

Klaus, E. 2022. Transitional Bodies, Party Politics, and Anti-democratic Potential in Tunisia. In M. Zayani (Ed.), *A Fledgling Democracy: Tunisia in the Aftermath of the Arab Uprisings* (pp. 59–85). C. Hurst & Co.

Rugh, W. A. 1979. *The Arab Press: News Media and Political Process in the Arab World*. Syracuse University Press.

Sakr, N. 2001. *Satellite Realms: Transnational Television, Globalization and the Middle East*. I B Tauris.

Sakr, N. 2007. *Arab Television Today*. I B Tauris.

Sakr, N. 2012. Book Review: Contemporary Arab Broadcast Media. *Cinema Journal*, 52(1), 176–178. https://doi.org/10.1353/cj.2012.0119 (accessed 15 July 2024).

Sakr, N. 2016. Book Review: Democracy's Fourth Wave? Digital Media and the Arab Spring. *The International Journal of Press/Politics*, 21(1), 136–137. https://doi.org/10.1177/1940161215611988 (accessed 15 July 2024).

Sakr, N. 2022. Media Governance as Diagnostic Lens to Probe Hidden Dimensions of Authoritarian Decision-Making in the Arab Middle East. In S.A. Ganter and H. Badr (Eds.), *Media Governance: A Cosmopolitan Critique* (pp. 39–57). Palgrave Macmillan.

Sakr, N. 2023. Purposes and Practices of MENA Television: Components of an Ever-Evolving Medium. In J. F. Khalil, G. Khiabany, T. Guaaybess and B. Yesil (Eds.), *The Handbook of Media and Culture in the Middle East* (pp. 122–133). Wiley Blackwell.

Springborg, R. 2020. *Political Economies of the Middle East & North Africa*. Polity Press.

Tawil-Souri, H. 2008. Arab Television in Academic Scholarship. *Sociology Compass*, 2(5), 1400–1415. https://doi.org/10.1111/j.1751-9020.2008.00155.x (accessed 15 July 2024).

Wilmsen, D. 2002. What Some of the Arab World is Watching. *Arab Media & Society*, June 1. https://www.arabmediasociety.com/what-some-of-the-arab-world-is-watching/ (accessed 15 July 2024).

CHAPTER 9

Beyond Whig Interpretation: Trends in Brazilian Media Histories

Otávio Daros

Power Without Responsibility is an attempt to renew the historiography of the press and broadcasting, whose tendency in recent decades has been towards increasing dialogue with the social sciences. In this sense, one of the merits of James Curran and Jean Seaton's undertaking is to present a far richer analysis of media history that contrasts with previous orthodox treatises of the process of development of communications that lack this interpretative sophistication.

The key element in this form of traditional historiography is that it offers a view of the present as overcoming the repressive past and inaugurating a new era of uninterrupted progress. This way of writing history—sometimes referred to as 'Whig history,' a term coined by Herbert Butterfield (1931)—can be characterised by its dualism, basically dividing the different subjects of the historical process into those, for example, who supported censorship policies and those who fought for press freedom.

Among the pioneering names in communication studies, a critique of this approach was outlined by James W. Carey in the 1970s. In an essay published in the debut issue of *Journalism History*, he called for a cultural turn for the discipline, possibly under the influence of reading of Clifford Geertz's anthropology essays. His understanding of communication as culture applied to the history of journalism meant shifting the focus from institutions or businesses to the text, especially reporting.

However, the criticism of Whig historiography by Curran and Seaton took place in other ways. Instead of symbolic anthropology, what we see here is a historical work that adopts political economy as a guide, reaffirming rather than leaving behind the understanding of the media as a set of institutions and its problematic nature as an enterprise, whether public or private. In place of communication as culture, the key notion here is that of power.

The aim of this chapter is to contribute to and problematise this picture of media historiography by introducing an overview of Brazilian scholarship. I begin by showing that, although early Brazilian histories share tendencies with English ones framed as Whiggish, the term must be used with care, otherwise it risks stereotyping the interpretations made by 19th-century newspaper historians. Next, the discussion turns to the works that emerged in Brazil in the second half of the 20th century onwards, in their relations with international trends in the renewal of media historiography, represented in the UK most notably by *Power Without Responsibility*.

Early historiography and the narrative of progress

The establishment of the press in Brazil took place in 1808 with the transfer of the Portuguese Royal Family to Rio de Janeiro, a situation that led to the founding of a gazette, the first periodical printed in the country. Until then, Brazil was a colony of the Portuguese empire which, among many other intellectual activities, prohibited in its territory in the Americas not only the opening of a university, but also the production of any printed word. Until independence in 1822, shortly before censorship was abolished, printing was a royal monopoly.

The birth of a historical intellectual production in Brazil is related to this process of formation of the nation state. Similar to more traditional branches of history, the study of the press emerged in the country only after the opening of the Brazilian Historical and Geographical Institute (IHGB) in 1838. No different than in most nations, in Brazil the writing of newspaper history was initially the initiative of journalists themselves, or publicists who, without distinguishing themselves from historians and biographers, at least until the turn of the 20th century, were still confused with politicians and the literati.

But like any historiography, this carries specificities of its time and space. A detailed examination of the body of writing produced by the pioneering generation of newspaper historians reveals a series of interpretative tendencies, which go far beyond what the Whig history framework usually suggests (see Daros 2023). Hence the importance of always analysing texts in light of their context, which includes the study of journalism research and theory.

One of the first aspects to note is that Brazilian press historiography reflects the experience generated by three centuries of colonisation. After independence, Portugal became the object of greater criticism by the intellectual elite that emerged in Brazil who blamed the absolutist and repressive regime for the delay in the arrival of the press in Portuguese America (e.g. Carvalho 1908). This was different to the situation in Spanish-speaking countries such as Mexico and Peru, which were introduced to Gutenberg's technology during the 16th century.

This approach was not liberal on the whole but conservative, as it challenged the partisan press for being agents of radicalisation and social division, while it idealised journalism as a means of promoting education and social cohesion across the nation. Early newspaper historians therefore tended to see the period in which political pamphleteering was dominant as a chapter in the history of the press that needed to be overcome. They sought to praise, on the other hand, the flowering of literary journalism, when the press began to incorporate values of neutrality and moderation (e.g. Moreira de Azevedo 1865).

Thus, the journalistic phenomenon is placed on a line of continuous development, in order to equate it with the successful cases of the press in England and France (Sousa Martins 1846). Such progress would have been achieved thanks to the promising conditions created during the reign of Dom Pedro II. This militancy through the writing of national history is ultimately related to the fact that the emperor was the patron and financier of the most traditional entity for preserving the country's memory.

Modern historiography and the narrative of underdevelopment

The tradition linked to the Brazilian Historical and Geographical Institute and its state counterparts began to decline during the first half of the 20th century. In the meantime, the first university institutions in the country were founded, notably the University of São Paulo (USP) and the Federal University of Rio de Janeiro (UFRJ). It should be noted, however, that historical works remained individual projects that were external to the university which, until the end of the 1960s, was basically a space for teaching rather than academic research.

Still, the press histories published in this transitional phase have important trends in relation to those from the 19th century. These accounts start to move away from a catalogue format that involved compiling data from every newspaper and magazine published in the country's former provinces. At the same time, grand narratives emerge that are less about inventory and more about interpretation (e.g. Barbosa Lima Sobrinho 1923), focusing on the formation of the mainstream press as a modern institution and the journalist as a professional information producer (e.g. Bahia 1960).

These books abandon the nativist approach that privileges only local periodicals and develop a more cosmopolitan view of the journalism. A consequence of this is that the history of Brazilian journalism starts to be framed in relation to foreign models and is basically divided into two major periods. The first is marked by the phase of political/literary journalism, represented by the Franco-European case while the second focuses on modern news journalism, represented by the Anglo-American experience (e.g. Freitas Nobre 1968). Hence there is a strong tendency to judge the national case based on international parameters, demanding, for example, the development of a press that is more objective than opinionated.

An influential voice during this period is that of Marxist historian Werneck Sodré (1966) who argued that although newspapers develop in line with technical progress, they thrive when political activity is more intense and varied. This understanding contrasts with that of previous historians who saw the era of political instability of the *pasquins*—openly partisan newspapers—as an undesirable chapter in the history of the press. For Sodré, on the contrary, these were the times when the press achieved its objective of serving as a means of struggle (Rüdiger and Daros 2022) in contrast to the contemporary phase of neoliberalism and media oligopolies, when journalism would mainly serve advertisers, divorcing itself from the public interest.

In short, modern narratives are no longer built around the idea of overcoming the cultural and economic backwardness of colonisation and securing progress with the establishment of an independent nation. Instead, narratives of journalism history emerged based on discussions linked to the country's intellectual and material dependence on other international powers and its underdevelopment, which poses obstacles to editorial and journalistic activities, limiting freedom of the press and access to information by the mass of the population.

New and varied media histories in recent times

The continuing development of media history studies in Brazil is part of a larger movement to expand postgraduate research from north to south in the country, through the creation of academic programmes in both the areas of history and communication. During the stage of institutionalisation of the field of knowledge between the 1970s and 1990s, there was a focus on media regulation, the transformation of newspapers into news industries and their role in national public opinion (Capelato and Prado 1980).

Since the turn of the 2000s, there has been a distancing in relation to Marxism, relegating the study of ideology to a secondary category. There has been a renewal of political history and, at the same time, an increase in cultural history which has certainly driven a shift from grand narratives to micro-histories and case studies with increasingly eclectic theoretical and methodological frameworks.

In this scenario, the media begin to be seen less as instruments of manipulation and much more in relation to an environment composed of varied practices of power and multiple cultural representations (Neves, Morel and Ferreira 2006). Since then, there has been a growing interest in issues linked to the relationship between image and identity, as well as the form and style of reporting. On the other hand, comparative international or transnational histories are still rare (e.g. Sousa et al. 2014).

Ultimately, the situation in Brazil largely echoes the point made by James Curran (2002) when studying the historiography of the British media that this is a tradition formed by a variety of approaches and narratives, but one that is generally limited to the individual study of mediums. Instead, we need to invest more in understanding changes across media landscapes and evaluate journalism's role in a broader social context using comparative research.

References

Bahia, J. 1960. *Três fases da imprensa brasileira*. Presença.

Barbosa Lima Sobrinho, A. J. 1923. *O problema da imprensa*. Álvaro Pinto.

Capelato, M. H., and Prado, M. L. 1980. *O bravo matutino: imprensa e ideologia no jornal 'O Estado de S. Paulo'*. Alfa-Ômega.

Carey, J. W. 1974. The Problem of Journalism History. *Journalism History*, 1(1), 3–27. https://doi.org/10.1080/00947679.1974.12066714

Carvalho, A. 1908. *Genese e progressos da imprensa periodica no Brazil*. IHGB.

Curran, J. 2002. Media and the Making of British Society, c. 1700–2000. *Media History*, 8(2), 135–154. https://doi.org/10.1080/1368880022000047137

Curran, J. and Seaton, J. 2018. *Power Without Responsibility: Press, Broadcasting and the Internet in Britain*, 8th edition. Routledge.

Daros, O. 2023. Prehistory of Journalism Studies: Discovering the Brazilian Tradition. *Journalism*, OnlineFirst, 1–17. https://doi.org/10.1177/14648849231200325

Freitas Nobre, J. 1968. *Lei da informação: lei de imprensa, rádio, televisão e agência de notícias*. Saraiva.

Moreira de Azevedo, M. D. 1865. Origem e desenvolvimento da imprensa no Rio de Janeiro. *Revista IHGB*, 29, 169–224.

Neves, L. M. B. P., Morel, M., and Ferreira, T. M. B. C. (Eds.), 2006. *História e imprensa: representações culturais e práticas de poder*. DP&A.

Rüdiger, F. and Daros, O. 2022. Marxist Thinking and Journalism Theory in Brazil. *Rethinking Marxism*, 34(4), 538–557. https://doi.org/10.1080/08935696.2022.2139079

Sodré, N. W. 1966. *História da imprensa no Brasil*. Civilização Brasileira.

Sousa, J. P., Lima, H., Hohlfeldt, A., and Barbosa, M. (Eds.), 2014. *History of the Press in the Portuguese-Speaking Countries*. Midia XXI.

Sousa Martins, F. 1846. Progresso do jornalismo no Brasil. *Revista IHGB*, 8, 262–275.

CHAPTER 10

Stamped and Unstamped Media in Contemporary Brazil

Afonso de Albuquerque

This chapter considers the contribution of Curran and Seaton's *Power Without Responsibility* (*PWR*) to international scholarship and, in particular, to that of my native country, Brazil. *PWR* is both provocative and rigorous. It contends that the hegemonic narrative on the history of the British press is more a mythology than an account supported by historical evidence. Four decades after it was originally published, *PWR* remains an indispensable source for those who want to know more about the history of the British news media, and the authors have continuously updated their book to cope with the social, political and technological changes that affected the British media since it first came out.

The hegemonic narrative of the history of UK journalism presents a tale of bravery and the love for freedom. According to this perspective and guided by these principles, since the mid-1600s, journalists in Britain have challenged state censorship and, progressively, made the freedom of the press a central principle of modern liberal democracies. The commercial nature of the press and advertising were instrumental in allowing them to be independent of political parties and the government. This narrative has dominated the landscape of journalism studies in the UK for more than a century. Its tremendous power has allowed UK journalism—and the US, which derives from it (Zelizer 2018)—to claim for themselves the role of setting the normative standards for journalism around the world. The manner in which the Fourth Estate—a term anchored in specificities of UK journalism history—became a synonym for journalism worldwide provides strong evidence in this regard. *PWR* presents a powerful critique of these romantic versions of the history of British journalism. Far from the unconditional love for abstract principles such as 'freedom', Curran and Seaton present the search for particular interests and privileges illustrating the double standards that come into play in the concrete application of abstract principles.

What lessons can *PWR* provide for scholars working outside the United Kingdom? The mythology of the development of the British news media has travelled abroad, often with the status of factual history. Journalists and scholars working in other societies often measure the concrete behaviour of their own country's press against an idealised image of the British media. It follows that they tend to consider their journalistic institutions inferior to those in Britain. This contributes to the tremendous normative authority the British media has in other countries.

PWR sheds light on multiple aspects of this mythology. This chapter focuses on two aspects in particular, which are discussed in the two first parts of *PWR*. Written by James Curran, the first part of the book presents a portrait of the history of the British press that contrasts vividly with the standard rosy account of a pathway towards ever-greater freedom and public responsibility. Curran demonstrates that the British press's love for freedom was conditional and subject to double standards. Freedom of the press did not come as a right for the entire press but as a privilege for the elite press. British politicians took all sorts of measures to undermine the viability of the popular press. They included laws on sedition and blasphemy, and taxes on knowledge.

A consequence of this move was the emergence of an unstamped press. Despite the risks involved in their publishing, the unstamped press was able to prosper for a time, but this only resulted in more repression. When newspaper taxes were repealed in the mid-1800s, the arguments justifying this movement were not all about freedom but also about control. In the view of many free press supporters, in the right hands, a cheap press could be an instrument for a more secure social order by securing, as Lord Palmerston says (quoted in *PWR*), 'the loyalty and good conduct of the lower classes' (Curran and Seaton 2018, 23).

Eventually, these measures were abandoned by the mid-19th century. However, by this time they had already been efficient in preventing the development of the radical press. This created favourable circumstances for the rise of a predominantly right-wing industrialised press and opened the way for the era of the press barons. In the following decades, the large press groups led by these media tycoons allowed them to exert huge political influence.

In the second part of the book, Jean Seaton explores the development of broadcasting in the UK. The British Broadcasting Corporation has been saluted as a model of quality television for the rest of the world. One of the core elements of the BBC's prestige abroad rests on its reputation for political impartiality. Yet, things are more complicated than this. On the one hand, the effort to build the BBC as a public broadcasting system presents a positive contribution as, at least in principle, it establishes public standards for producing media content. This contrasts vividly with the tradition of the British commercial newspapers, serving their proprietors' own vested interests. On the other hand, in practical terms, the BBC's autonomy regarding the government is much more limited than commonsense views would have us believe.

How do these considerations apply to journalism in Brazil? As happened in the UK, Brazil also developed its own tradition of 'press barons'. The family-owned elite press gained special importance after World War II. They firmly opposed initiatives aimed at giving labour rights to the working class, labelling them 'populistic'. They did not hesitate to foster political instability in defence of their political interests. For example, in 1954, they led an uprising against their archenemy, the social reformer President Getúlio Vargas. Feeling helpless, Vargas opted to take his own life rather than acquiesce to his opponents' demands and renounce his post. Ten years later, in 1964, the legacy press provided political support for a coup d'état against President João Goulart, who also intended to promote social reforms. A military dictatorship followed that lasted until 1985.

Brazilian legacy media often presents itself as a champion of freedom of expression but, as in the UK, their defence of this principle uses double standards. The Brazilian mainstream press has historically been concentrated in a few hands and is elite-oriented. The family oligarchies that dominate the market champion conservative values and see the press as an exclusive club to be defended against outsiders. In 1951, Samuel Wainer created *Última Hora*, a newspaper aligned with Getúlio Vargas who, as stated above, was hated by the mainstream media. It soon became tremendously popular. The reaction of the Brazilian press barons was furious. They threw doubt on Wainer's nationality, accusing him of being a Bessarabian—i.e. from the region now in Moldovia—and not Brazilian even though he was a native of São Paulo. For this reason, they claimed he was not fit to own a newspaper in Brazil, according to the law. Initially, they failed. Still, the pressure against *Última Hora* persisted and it finally closed its doors in 1971, during the military regime. The political and economic pressure faced by *Última Hora* proved to be too much. In the eyes of the Brazilian elites and legacy media, *Última Hora* lacked the 'stamp' of respectability that would have allowed it to carry on being published.

Unlike the UK, public service never played a significant role in the Brazilian broadcasting system. In Brazil, both radio and television have been dominated by commercial stations. For decades, the technology to allow nationwide broadcasting was not available in Brazil. Radio and television stations worked exclusively on a local basis, which significantly reduced their political influence. This changed in 1969, when the Brazilian government provided a satellite infrastructure for television broadcasting. Globo Television Network took advantage of this infrastructure to build a privately owned quasi-monopoly in Brazil. It follows that the 'press baron' logic went on to dominate Brazilian television as well as the press.

In a general manner, the legacy media supported the military dictatorship in return for economic benefits. This happened despite being subjected to censorship and many journalists being subjected to harassment, prison and even torture by the regime. However, when it became obvious that the military regime was experiencing a terminal crisis in the mid-1980s, they changed sides and presented themselves as deeply committed to the new democratic order. During the first two decades of the new democratic era, the legacy media maintained close relationships with the government. Then, these media—and Globo Network above all—were so influential that they considered themselves working as a quasi-official fourth branch of the government (Albuquerque 2005). At that time, the legacy media played a pivotal role in the defence of the neoliberal reforms in the late 1990s and early 2000s.

All this changed after the Workers' Party (Partido dos Trabalhadores [PT]) managed to elect Luis Inácio Lula da Silva as president of Brazil in 2002. He won an additional term in 2006, and his fellow party member Dilma Rousseff won two consecutive elections in 2010 and 2014. Never had a single political party won four elections in a row in Brazil. Social policies intended to reduce poverty were the main reason for this success. Similar to what occurred with Getúlio Vargas, five decades before, the legacy media accused the PT governments of benefiting from populist measures and denounced them as being fundamentally anti-democratic (Albuquerque and Gagliardi 2020).

As this happened, the legacy media became more and more frustrated and assumed an increasingly oppositional attitude towards the federal government. According to Maria Judith Brito, the president of Associação Nacional de Jornais (National Newspaper Association), the legacy news media was becoming the de facto political opposition to the government, a role that the opposition parties were no longer able to fulfil. They were especially critical of Lula's intention to create a competitive public television sector that was inspired by the BBC model. For the privately owned broadcasting companies, such a move demonstrated an intent to establish authoritarian control over information by PT-supporting governors.

In 2010, a group of progressive journalists joined efforts to create an alternative to legacy media, aiming to provide some degree of external pluralism to news media coverage: they took advantage of the new opportunities provided by the emergence of digital media. As has happened in the past, conservative politicians and the legacy media reacted bitterly to the advent of such competitors, calling them 'dirty blogs' and denying their status as journalists.

During the 2010s, the Brazilian legacy media engaged in progressively divisive behaviour in the political sphere. Incapable of defeating PT by electoral means, they provided support for alternative means to remove PT from the presidency. They systematically associated PT with corruption and even depicted it as a 'criminal organisation' (Albuquerque and Gagliardi 2020). This climate of political polarisation and generalised suspicion led Rousseff's second presidential term to end abruptly after a controversial impeachment process. Many analysts considered this to be unconstitutional because the Brazilian Constitution states that impeachment should only apply in cases where presidents commit serious crimes, and there were no criminal accusations pending against President Rousseff. Vice-president Michel Temer, who replaced her, soon implemented a series of neoliberal reforms with the firm backing of the legacy media. At that time, and unlike his predecessor, Temer was, in fact, facing criminal accusations related to corruption. In 2017, Judge Sergio Moro sentenced former president Lula to prison under corruption charges related to Lava Jato, a major anticorruption judicial operation. Lula was sent to jail the following year. Further evidence revealed numerous irregularities in the criminal process against Lula. In 2019, the Brazilian Supreme Court ordered him to be released, and in the following years, all accusations against him were dropped. The divisive behaviour of the legacy media cost them considerable prestige at that time.

Lula's arrest prevented him from running in the 2018 presidential election and paved the way for Jair Bolsonaro's victory. A far-right, anti-institutional politician, Bolsonaro benefited from the climate of political polarisation and suspicion towards the democratic institutions prevailing at that time. To be sure, Bolsonaro was not the dream candidate for the legacy media owners but at that moment, he was preferable to Fernando Haddad who replaced Lula as the PT's candidate.

Ironically enough, Bolsonaro's hostility towards the legacy press surpassed by far that demonstrated by his PT predecessors. Moreover, during the 2018 electoral campaign and his presidential term, Bolsonaro and the alt-right media supporting him systematically fostered political polarisation, cast doubt on the political institutions, and spread disinformation as part of their political strategy. This proved especially disastrous during the Covid-19 pandemic.

Bolsonaro's chaotic government provided the legacy media with a fresh opportunity to look respectable again. They rebranded themselves as a part of a disinformation-fighting system that adopts a multistakeholder approach. In this model, fact-checking agencies were supposed to detect disinformation and identify the agents disseminating it. Social media platforms then punished these outlets by restricting their visibility or even banning them with the prospect of further sanctions from the judiciary.

In this schema, the legacy media was supposed to be the a priori disseminator of trustworthy information. This meant that claims presented by the legacy media were never subjected to checking, and they therefore remained exempt from any disinformation-related sanctions. Here, it is worth noting that news (that subsequently proved to be false) published by the legacy media played a crucial role in convincing public opinion that Lula was guilty of corruption and therefore deserved to be imprisoned. Needless to say, the fact-checking agencies never scrutinised these claims.

I argue that this system revives the historical logic of the stamped media as described in *PWR*. Under the pretext of curbing disinformation spread by alt-right media, it stigmatises everything that is not mainstream, including the progressive news media. On some occasions, fact-checking agencies have classified news published by progressive media outlets as fake news, leading these media to be punished by social media platforms with a temporary ban or decreased visibility. A blatant case occurred on 12 June 2018, when the alternative news site, *Revista Forum*, published an article saying that Pope Francis had sent Lula (who was in jail at the time) a chaplet and a letter as an expression of solidarity. Other media, both alternative and mainstream, reproduced this claim. The fact-checking agency Lupa promptly classified the information as fake news and recommended that Facebook punish the alternative media as spreaders of disinformation. This did not happen with the legacy media that published the same information. Later, the information proved to be true.

All in all, this 'truth verification' system works as a functional equivalent of the British stamping scheme described in *PWR*. Using the excuse of protecting 'respectable' journalism, it ostracises and marginalises progressive views while endowing conservative news with the status of 'common sense'.

References

Albuquerque, A. 2005. Another Fourth Branch: Press and Political Culture in Brazil. *Journalism*, 6(4), 486–504.

Albuquerque, A. and Gagliardi, J. 2020. Democracy as Corruption: The News Media and the Debunking of Democracy in Brazil. In X. Orchard et al. (Eds.) *Media & Governance in Latin America: Towards a Plurality of Voices* (pp. 77–96). Peter Lang.

Zelizer, B. 2018. Resetting Journalism in the Aftermath of Brexit and Trump. *European Journal of Communication*, 33(2), 140–156.

Part II

Market Impoverishment

Maintaining a Critical Tradition of Situating Media Within Wider Power Relations

Aeron Davis

I first came across *Power Without Responsibility* in Foyles bookshop in Charing Cross Road in 1993. I had decided to do an MA in the relatively new discipline of media studies. Having narrowed my choices down to a couple of programmes I wanted to get reading. Fittingly, my choice of MA programmes came down to either Goldsmiths, where James Curran was based, or Westminster, where Jean Seaton resided. At the time Foyles barely had a single bookcase devoted to Media, but it did have a whole shelf entitled 'Curran'. In between what were to become classic texts, such as *Mass Media and Society* (1991) and *Bending Reality* (1986), sat the third edition of *PWR* (1988).

I started reading. Not just Curran and Seaton, of course. They were two amongst several media and communication scholars (Garnham, Schlesinger, Hall, Murdock, Chomsky, Miege, McRobbie and others) who had been defining critical approaches to the field since its inception. Reading them enticed me into the subject. They helped explain to me something I instinctively knew then but could not explain how; that news media did not simply reflect the world as it is and, in fact, was deeply implicated in unequal power relations in modern societies. That Curran shelf led me to Goldsmiths' Department of Media and Communications, an MA and then PhD under James's supervision.

PWR was there at the start of my postgraduate journey and remains with me now. Through the late 1990s, I was a tutor on James Curran's undergraduate media history course, teaching the fourth edition. My PhD and first book (Davis 2002) cites the fifth edition while my most recent book (Davis 2024) references the eighth. Different editions have found their way onto a diverse set of my course reading lists covering media history, news and society, promotional cultures and political communication.

The book was just as relevant to many of my varied research projects. It, along with other works by Curran, helped me think about the many ways news media, popular culture and digital communication come to be intertwined with power. How a mix of unconscious economic and market forces, and more conscious political and corporate agency, shape content in ways that advantage the wealthy and powerful. When first reading the book, I understood much more about the multiple influences that skew the shape of news, popular culture and media content. From press barons and corporate boards to government interventions and regulations, they all contribute to an array of 'top-down influences' (Curran 2002) that include, but go beyond, the five filters of Herman and Chomsky's propaganda model (1988).

I was particularly struck by the multiple, hidden influences of advertising, past and present. Adverts didn't merely sell commodities: advertising altered news content and news markets. It caused journalists and editors to self-censor for fear of powerful advertiser comeback. Thus, it contributed to the framing of stories in particular ways or the exclusion of certain topics altogether. News brands and reporting topics were oriented towards recognised audience demographics that advertisers wanted to reach. At different points *PWR* explains how a lack of advertising was a fundamental cause of the decline of the UK working-class press in the middle of the 20th century; how this contributed to the dumbing-down and depoliticisation of much broadcast content in the late 20th century; and also how the winding down of national public service media is being justified by global market forces in the early 21st century.

I didn't end up researching advertising for my PhD but, instead, one of its related promotional professions: public relations. If advertising provides an essential direct economic subsidy for news, public relations offers an equivalent 'information subsidy' (Gandy 1982) for it. The two professions have much in common and many of those observations in *PWR* about advertising helped me think through how PR might equally shape news content and wider public discourse. As with advertising, it is powerful and well-resourced corporate and state entities that spend most here. Both attempt, with mixed results, to persuade all manner of audiences to particular understandings of the world, whether those relate to consumption, taste, personal gratifications or who to vote for.

Early editions of *PWR* were a lot slimmer and preoccupied with the history of print and limited terrestrial channel broadcasting in Britain. But, with each new edition, came new communications media: first multi-channel TV, then digital platforms, alternative and social media. So too, the focus grew more macro, linking to wider socioeconomic and political forces and global communication networks, as a now much larger volume adapted to changes both in society and communication.

The observations once applied only to newsprint media are equally applicable to broadcasting, platform capitalism, search engines and social media. The age of the press barons may be over, but they have been replaced by far more powerful, tech giant equivalents (Srnicek 2016; Hindman 2018). Amazon's founder Jeff Bezos snapped up the *Washington Post*, while Elon Musk has turned Twitter into X, his personal online fiefdom and propagator of mainly far-right and libertarian views. Mark Zuckerberg's Meta encompasses Facebook, Instagram and WhatsApp. They, along with other communication CEOs (Gates, Ellison, Page and Brin), dominate the list of the richest individuals in the world (Oxfam 2023).

Advertising algorithms now drive the activities of platforms, and the journalists and editors of alternative news providers and legacy media (Elvested and Phillips 2018; Benkler et al. 2018; Freelon and Wells 2020), are all increasingly drawn to the partisan, extreme and emotional content and headlines that gain clicks and shares.

Just as *PWR* helped me think about how advertising and promotional culture shape media and cultural content, so it also contributed to my thinking about politics, political communication and elites. Unlike many other media texts and communication studies, *PWR* is not media-centric or techno-determinist in its approach. The evolution of British media is situated within its historical context. Communication is embedded in wider socioeconomic relations, networks, politics and power relations. Communication media both enable and constrain, structure and give agency, offer alternatives and assist consolidation of status quo forces and institutions, and facilitate both transformation and normalisation.

PWR, like many great historical and sociopolitical analyses of power and society, insists that media, communication and culture are seen as embedded in structures and networks of hegemonic influence. Thus, C. Wright Mills' classic on the power elite (1956), noted the role of media elites and content in the establishment of the American military industrial complex. Stephen Lukes (1974) argued that an all-important third dimension of power was ideological, reproduced through media (non) reporting. Pierre Bourdieu (1979) regularly came back to media and culture as part of larger discussions of inequality. All were drawn to media's role without engaging with critical media studies.

So, it is to Curran and Seaton along with such authors, that I look to decipher how modern politics and elite power both influence and are influenced by modern media and communication. This is significant at a time when the departments and journals of the fields of political communication and journalism studies are increasingly apolitical. Guided as they are by empiricism and advanced quantitative (and computer-aided) research methods, they devote little space to critical theory and issues of power and inequality (Davis et al. 2020; Phelan and Maeseele 2023).

This gap is important. In many wealthy democracies, it is far too evident that the ownership of media and communication infrastructure, as well as the advertising and other information subsidies that feed them, are linked to money, big business and national politics. In the 2020 US election, total campaign expenditure for all candidates topped $14.4 billion, with the biggest area of expenditure being political advertising. In 2021, registered lobbyists spent $3.78 billion, over 90% of which came from corporate advocacy operations (Open Secrets 2021, 2022). Drutman (2015) recorded that a third of senators who step down from politics join such firms. In recent years, the big Silicon Valley tech companies have become some of the largest spenders on lobbying worldwide. In 2022, four of the five largest-spending lobbyists in the EU came from the sector (Lobby Facts 2022). The big platforms are now fully involved in election campaigns providing key services to parties in multiple nations (Kreiss and McGregor 2018).

Beyond the US, no democracies expend anything like such vast sums. But the same links between media, lobbying, public relations, national politics and big business are still evident. In Aotearoa-New Zealand, where I have lived for the last three years, the per capita funding of its public news media compares very poorly to most wealthy democracies (Pickard 2019), and news outlet dependency on corporate advertising and public relations material is particularly high. Senior political figures move rapidly between being party managers and advisors and the corporate lobby sector. Between 2021 and 2023, the conservative National Party gained almost eight times as much in corporate donations as the Labour Party. The small, libertarian ACT Party, promoting radical tax cuts and a far-right agenda, gained four times as much in corporate donations and spent twice as much on social media advertising as Labour (Hancock 2023). The first acts of the new National-ACT-NZ First coalition have been to repeal a series of worker, environmental, renter and Māori-supporting legislation, while implementing tax cuts and deregulation that will benefit the wealthy and its big corporate donors, such as the property sector.

In the decades since that first edition of *PWR*, there have been many critical scholars and important texts. Many of them explore nations, histories, forms of communication media and research questions that *PWR* does not. But so many also acknowledge the significance of the text to their thinking and directions. In my case, although rarely writing about news journalism these days, the book remains as relevant as ever to my work on power, politics and inequality.

References

Benkler, Y., Faris, R. and Roberts, H. 2018. *Network Propaganda: Manipulation, Disinformation, and Radicalization in American Politics*. Oxford University Press.

Bourdieu, P. 1979. *Distinction*. Routledge.

Curran, J. 2002. *Media and Power*. Routledge.

Curran, J. and Gurevitch, M. (Eds.) 1991. *Mass Media and Society*. Arnold.

Curran, J., Ecclestone, J., Oakley, G. and Richardson, A. (Eds.) 1986. *Bending Reality: The State of the Media*. Pluto Press.

Davis, A. 2002. *Public Relations Democracy: Public Relations, Politics and the Mass Media in Britain*. Manchester University Press.

Davis, A. 2024. *Political Communication: An Introduction for Crisis Times*, 2nd edition. Polity Press.

Davis, A., Fenton, N., Freedman, D. and Khiabany, G. 2020. *Media, Democracy and Social Change: Re-Imagining Political Communication*. Sage.

Drutman, L. 2015. *The Business of America is Lobbying: How Corporations Became Politicized and Politics Became More Corporate*. Oxford University Press.

Elvestad, E. and Phillips, A. 2018. *Misunderstanding News Audiences: Seven Myths of the Social Media Era*. Routledge.

Freelon, D. and Wells, C. 2020. Disinformation as Political Communication. *Political Communication*, 37(2), 145–156.

Gandy, O. 1982. *Beyond Agenda Setting: Information Subsidies and Public Policy*. Ablex Publishing Corporation.

Hancock, F. 2023. National Banks 7.5 Times More in Donations Than Labour. *RNZ News* 23 August. Available at: https://www.rnz.co.nz/news/in-depth/496383/national-banks-7-point-5-times-more-in-donations-than-labour.

Herman, E. and Chomsky, N. 1988. *Manufacturing Consent: The Political Economy of the Mass Media*. Pantheon.

Hindman, M. 2018. *The Internet Trap: How the Digital Economy Builds Monopolies and Undermines Democracy*. Princeton University Press.

Kreiss, D. and McGregor, S. 2018. Technology Firms Shape Political Communication: The Work of Microsoft, Facebook, Twitter, and Google With Campaigns During the 2016 U.S. Presidential Cycle. *Political Communication*, 35(2), 155–177.

LobbyFacts 2022. https://www.lobbyfacts.eu

Lukes, S. 1974. *Power: A Radical View*. Palgrave Macmillan.

Mills, C. W. 1956. *The Power Elite*. Oxford University Press.

OpenSecrets 2021, 2022. https://www.opensecrets.org

Oxfam 2023. *Survival of the Richest*. Oxfam.

Phelan, S. and Maeseele, P. 2023. Where is 'the Political' in the Journal *Political Communication*? On the Hegemonic Articulation of a Disciplinary Identity. *Annals of the International Communication Association*, 47(2), 202–221.

Pickard, V. 2019. *Democracy Without Journalism? Confronting the Misinformation Society*. Oxford University Press.

Srnicek, N. 2016. *Platform Capitalism*. Polity.

CHAPTER 12

Market Impoverishment, Democratic Choices

Jonathan Hardy

My first copy of *Power Without Responsibility*, from 1988, took me on a journey, not only to becoming a media academic, but also secretary of the Campaign for Press Broadcasting Freedom, a socialist media reform group that James Curran helped to establish in the late 1970s. So, my thoughts on market impoverishment are also a reflection on the arguments used in campaigning and policy advocacy over a long period of communications deregulation, better described as liberalising re-regulation in favour of commercial market actors.

PWR traces the bifurcation in British media policy and market arrangements between a free-market (but still state subsidised) press and a regulated broadcasting system that combined public service media, notably the BBC, with regulated but commercially funded media. The first edition, in 1981, reflects a key moment that anchors the book, when this mixed system started to give way to deeper marketisation and liberalisation, and, from the 1990s, to the new market actors of the internet era.

James Curran's work certainly highlights market impoverishment, but I would argue the general position can be described as **market insufficiency**. It is important to note that this is not a totalistic critique of market provision. A total critique would flatten differences that his work explores—how commercialism may shape and sometimes dominate media, but can also be mixed with other purposes: professionalism, widening cultural expression, serving communities, even public service.

In a similar way Robert McChesney's (1999) use of the term hypercommercialism was intended to identify when the balancing of profit-seeking and other influences on media content production tipped decisively toward commercial values—for instance, towards what McManus (1994) called market-driven journalism. So, Curran's work displays a historian's sensibility to investigate, rather than pronounce a priori, how forces of commercialism have interacted with other forces to shape media, usually in complex and contradictory ways.

The second feature is an acknowledgement of merits in market provision, which I would describe as **the market as supplementary**. This informs Curran's influential model of a mixed media system; one that proposes a core public service sector encircled by a *private sector*, the commercial market, a *social market sector* that subsidises media providers to enhance plurality, and *professional* and *civil media* sectors (Curran 2002). Creating a dynamic disequilibria, the various sectors influence each other and are mutually enhancing to strengthen media independence, increase diversity and generate quality. This normative model was constructed to address problems in Anglo-American media systems, but it provides a versatile framework for more international and comparative studies, as developed in his later work.

In the edited collection, *De-westernising Media Studies* (Curran and Park 2000), close attention is paid by invited authors to conditions in which market provision was a positive force for progressive democratic and social change. So, here is a third account of the market as a pro-social force, under certain conditions; marking space for what Curran (2001) called intermediate positions between free-market ideology and market critique. Yet, certainly in his own work, that positive assessment was heavily contingent on context. *De-Westernizing Media Studies* also included numerous studies of private market actors closely enmeshed with authoritarian political and economic systems, across post-communist Russia, and Mexico, for instance. These accounts demonstrate that the free market is no guarantor of editorial independence and show privately owned media as cheerleaders for mutually supportive political elites.

Such illiberal mutuality is also illustrated in the UK, where Rupert Murdoch's *Sun* failed to join media investigations in 2021–22 into the then-Prime Minister Boris Johnson's breaches of Covid-19 lockdown rules, while Murdoch lobbied successfully to rescind the undertaking he was required to sign in 1981 (note the date), to guarantee editorial independence for, and between, *The Times* and *The Sunday Times* (Waterson 2022).

Curran's work is in a critical tradition that challenges myths of the market. This is a key area that relates to my own work on advertising. The core argument is that ad-dependent media markets serve advertiser interests as well as consumers, problematising the notion that market provision is an expression of popular will. The idealised notion of market democracy ignores the structuring influence of advertising. The skewing of media finance, notably advertising, to favour commercially valuable audiences and disfavour others, results in certain information and cultural expressions being privileged, while others may be rendered invisible. It is fitting that James Curran was the first winner of the C. Edwin Baker award (2011), as both scholars emphasise that market impoverishment is not just a matter of supply shaped by commercial imperatives, but the insufficiency of market mechanisms to register or respond to preferences (Baker 1994, 2002, 2007).

My own work has focused on branded content—content funded or produced by marketers—and this certainly highlights, if not always new, at least intensifying varieties of market impoverishment (Hardy 2022a). The context is one of brands as the self-styled patrons of communications, and brand invasion of media content: sponsored content in news media; product integration in audiovisual, influencer marketing and native advertising across social media.

Consider the debate we are currently having in the UK about whether the Netflix model is sufficient to replace the BBC. Netflix is deeply involved, like other streaming services, in brand integration in their original productions. Research from 2018 found that 100% of Amazon's original programming contained brand integrations, 91% of Hulu and 74% of Netflix originals (Tran 2018). Netflix carries an increasing amount of brand funded content such as Patagonia's documentary *Artifishal* (2019), but also content that is brand funded but appears unbranded to many viewers. And there is a complex dalliance between Netflix's brand partnership group and brands who want to reach its young, upscale audience. In 2019, Netflix's *Stranger Things* did deals with 75 brands. Netflix was arguably more interested in cross-promotion through brand partnerships than product placement revenues, but it is deeply enmeshed with its own and others' brand promotion in ways that are contractually agreed between the parties but not fully disclosed and transparent to the rest of us.

From examples such as these, I want to make a broader argument that we need to develop further the critique of market impoverishment as a **critique of governance**. This is a critique of the lack of accountability and governance oversight of market actors.

Governance is a very useful (if slippery) concept—attending to all processes that shape rules affecting behaviour (Hardy 2022b). Applied to branded content this includes the various weaknesses in governance, from formal regulation to industry self-regulation, that result in a lack of transparency about brand funding and brand control over communications content and services. I will illustrate this by way of two paradoxes. The first is that since 1966 the leading international code of advertising (first created in 1937 by the International Chamber of Commerce) has clear rules on identification: ads should be 'clearly distinguishable as such' (ICC 1966, 2018). Yet since then, we have had waves of integrated and disguised ads (Hardy 2022a). The second paradox, situated within the first, is that there has been increasing regulatory attention, in America since 2015, in Australia, UK and across Europe, yet massive non-observance.

The UK Advertising Standards Authority reported in March 2021 on its analysis of over 24,000 posts by 122 UK-based influencers which revealed 'a disappointing overall rate of compliance with the rules on making it sufficiently clear when they were being paid to promote a product or service' (Advertising Standards Authority 2021, 3); 65% were non-compliant. Similarly, Australia's self-regulator Ad Standards (2021) found widespread breaches of its code.

So, I want to argue for *developing* the critique of market impoverishment as a critique of accountability and governance. Now this is certainly not new, as critiques of the 'unfettered' free-markets makes clear. But if we compare communications today with the conditions at the time of the first edition of *PWR*, the lack of accountability and democratic governance loom even larger as features to be addressed: the rise of unaccountable, private, corporate actors. This point has been made powerfully by many people, including Vincent Mosco (2014) in his book *To the Cloud* on the new digital giants. Contrast today with the UK media system in 1981 when a *regulated* media market included and influenced all market actors, with public provision acting as check and spur for quality of market provision creating a kind of balanced system (narrow in politics and culture—but with Channel Four, which launched in 1982, about to add greater diversity).

So, my key argument is that *market impoverishment* is, amongst other things, the *impoverishment of governance*. If private actors are to provide communication services vital to the public sphere, for cultural diversity and exchange—what should be the appropriate governance arrangements?

What should connect market *power* with *responsibility* to the social realm? And that means that the linked tasks of analysis and action—gathering the research to try to inform citizens and influence the direction of policy and governance arrangements—remains as important as it has ever been to the authors of *PWR*. It also makes central their call for a regulatory state that is the means by which democratic forces—in their long historical view, the organised working class and new social movements—can push back against unaccountable market actors to create a mixed media system with advertiser-free, public service media at its core. We are indebted to Curran and Seaton for their inspiring guidance.

References

Ad Standards 2021. Updates to AiMCO's Influencer Marketing Code of Practice, 25 August. https://adstandards.com.au/article/updates-aimco's-influencer-marketing-code-practice

Advertising Standards Authority. 2021. *Influencer Ad Disclosure on Social Media.* https://www.asa.org.uk/static/dd740667-6fe0-4fa7-80de3e4598417912/Influencer-Monitoring-Report-March2021.pdf

Baker, C. E. 1994. *Advertising and a Democratic Press.* Princeton University Press.

—— 2002. *Media, Markets, and Democracy.* Cambridge University Press.

—— 2007. *Media Concentration and Democracy.* Cambridge University Press.

Curran, J. 2001. Media Regulation in the Era of Market Liberalism. In G. Philo and D. Miller (Eds.) *Market Killing: What the Free Market Does and What Social Scientists Can do About It* (pp. 216–232). Longman.

—— 2002. Media and Democracy: The Third Way. In *Media and Power* (pp. 217–247). Routledge.

——and Seaton, J. (1981/1988/2018) *Power Without Responsibility: Press, Broadcasting and the Internet in Britain.* Routledge.

—— and Park, M-J. (Eds.) 2000. *De-Westernising Media Studies.* Routledge.

Hardy, J. 2022a. *Branded Content: The Fateful Merging of Media and Marketing.* Routledge.

—— 2022b. Meeting the Challenges of Media and Marketing Convergence: Revising Critical Political Economy Approaches. In P. McDonald (Ed.) *The Routledge Companion to Media Industries* (pp. 55–65). Routledge.

ICC (International Chamber of Commerce) 1966. *International Code of Advertising Practice.* Paris: ICC.

ICC. 2018. *Advertising and Marketing Communications Code.* Paris: ICC. https://iccwbo.org/publication/icc-advertising-and-marketing-communications-code/

McChesney, R. 1999. *Rich Media, Poor Democracy: Communication Politics in Dubious Times.* University of Illinois Press.

McManus, J. H. 1994. *Market-Driven Journalism: Let the Citizens Beware?* Sage.

Mosco, V. 2014. *To the Cloud: Big Data in a Turbulent World*. Routledge.

Patagonia 2019. *Artifishal*. Dir. Liars and Thieves. https://eu.patagonia.com/gb/en/stories/artifishal/video-79192.html

Tran, K. 2018. OTT services are helping to drive product placement deals. *Business Insider*, 18 June. https://www.businessinsider.com/amazon-hulu-netflix-driving-product-placement-deals-2018-6?IR=T

Waterson, J. 2022. Ban on Rupert Murdoch's Interference in *Times* and *Sunday Times* ended. *The Guardian* (10 February). https://www.theguardian.com/media/2022/feb/10/ban-on-rupert-murdochs-interference-in-times-and-sunday-times-ended

CHAPTER 13

Power Without Responsibility:
Legacy and Lessons

Dwayne Winseck

James Curran and Jean Seaton's *Power Without Responsibility* (PWR) is a seminal text that has influenced generations of media scholars and observers since the 1980s, including this author. Revised and updated ever since, the ninth edition was published in 2025, and it continues to challenge orthodoxies while brimming with lessons regarding the ascendant power of digital platforms such as Google and Facebook on the internet today.

In what follows, I briefly reprise three themes in *PWR* that stand out for me, while adding a fourth that I believe deserves greater prominence than Curran and Seaton give to it:

1. The commercialisation of the press and the demise of the radical press.
2. The industrialisation of the press and media from the mid-19th century onwards.
3. The forms of media that we have is a function of politics, power and policy choices. Today, this takes the form of an urgent question we now face: what kind of internet, communications and digital media system do we want and who decides?
4. The media and cultural industries have always developed in very close proximity to much larger big tech, telecommunications, industrial and banking sectors, and have been subordinated to them (although never fully) since the mid-19th century.

The Commercialisation of the Press

Every edition of *PWR* begins by announcing the authors' bold intentions: 'This book attacks the conventional history of the press as a story of progress' (Curran and Seaton 2018, i) … 'an orthodoxy that lasted hundreds of years' (3). The authors make good their promise.

In the conventional history of the press that Curran and Seaton target, the removal of stamp taxes in the UK in the 1850s paved the way for the 'free press'. This was indeed important, they agree, but for different reasons than the ones usually stated. Rather than marking the permanent retreat of the state in favour of the free market and the free press, the elimination of stamp taxes was part and parcel of three decades of political and social upheaval in the UK and across Europe when working-class politics took root, along with the advent of a vibrant working-class press. Well-established elites and comfortable liberals trembled as a result, but simultaneously they took stern and sweeping measures to protect their power and privileges. Removing stamp taxes was one such measure.

Contra liberal Whig theories of the free press, the removal of the stamp taxes had three main aims:

a. To undercut the successes of the 'unstamped' radical press while actively promoting the development of the commercial press in 'responsible hands.'
b. To advance political socialisation efforts designed to bring the working and lower classes into the political fold and undercut the rebellions and uprisings taking place across Europe in 1848.
c. To legitimate the commercialisation of the press and political socialisation of the lower classes by wrapping both, late in the game, in the noble garb of liberal free press theory.

To this list, I would also like to add a fourth aspect that Curran and Seaton do not address: the British and US governments adopted major *communication* policy measures to aid the rise of the commercial press. In the UK, this took the form of 'cheap telegraph rates' and that policy goal was integral to the nationalisation of the telegraph system in 1868. In the US, the Postal Act of 1792 promoted the creation of the postal news exchange system that allowed newspaper and magazine publishers to exchange copies of their publications with other publishers as often as they liked free of charge, all with the aim of bringing 'general intelligence' to every person's doorstep.

The subsidies involved in the latter were worth billions of dollars per year (in inflation-adjusted dollars) (John 1998, 164-167).

In short, contra the myth of the free press that assumes that governments have been forever barred from intervening in the workings of the press for the last two hundred years, and that this is a bedrock principle of liberal democracy, the UK and US governments, in fact, adopted major public policies that leveraged control over communications infrastructure and public money to promote the development of the commercial press.

The industrialisation of the press

As the commercial press expanded, the industrialisation of the press was driven by the massive increase in the capital needed to establish a modern big city newspaper, to invest in printing presses and distribution, and to procure local, national and international news that made up the final product called 'the news'. Such processes and dynamics, however, differed between different societies.

Curran and Seaton, of course, examine the situation in the UK. Long before their work, however, Karl Bücher and Edwin Ross described such processes in Germany and the US. Bücher, an economist, referred to the modern press as a 'capitalistic enterprise, a sort of news-factory within which a great number of people… are employed on wage, under a single administration, at very specialized work' (quoted in Hardt 2001, 90). Edwin Ross, an American sociologist trained in the German economic historian tradition, and an early founding figure in media and communication studies in the US, described developments in similar terms. According to both, the industrialised press was characterised by three features: first, the steady eclipse of press barons by the rise of shareholder-owned capitalistic enterprises; second, the drift of media control into the hands of corporate interests driven more by business motives than political ambitions (1); and, third, the sharply rising costs for the necessary plant and news wire franchises, both of which drove press concentration in one city after another.

The speed and precise details regarding the commercialisation and industrialisation of the press varied significantly across time and place.

If we define the commercialised press as one where more than half of all revenue came from advertising rather than subscription fees, patronage, public subsidies or some other form, we can observe the following:

- In the UK, advertising revenue had come to account for, on average, two-thirds of quality broadsheet papers' revenue by the mid-1930s (Curran and Seaton 2003, 45).
- In the US, on average, the press saw advertising revenue grow from 44% in 1880 to surpass the 50% mark in the early 1890s and peaked at 82% in the early 2000s before slipping back to 44% by 2020 (Pickard 2022, personal correspondence).
- In Germany, the 50% of revenue from advertising bar was passed around 1910 (Bücher, cited in Hardt 2001, 90).
- In Canada, the commercialisation of the press was locked in sometime in the 1920s or 1930s (Sotiron 1997, 4–7).

These differences reveal the varieties of capitalism in play across time and place, then and now. They also remind us, in sharp contrast to Horkheimer and Adorno's (1947) culture industry thesis, that the industrialisation of culture, while certainly well underway when they were writing, was and has never been as complete as they assert. To its credit, Curran and Seaton's work alerts us to the perils of over-drawing a monochromatic critique of the media through their empirically rich history, contemporary political economy and culturally informed accounts of the media in the UK, and their insistence that the shape of the media systems we encounter—past and present—ultimately turns on politics, power and policy choices rather than the brute force of industrial and economic imperatives alone. Similar kinds of observations have also defined the work of successive generations of scholars who make up the Cultural Industries School (e.g. Miege 1989; Hesmondhalgh 2019).

The cultural industries grow in the shadows of 'big tech'

I want to turn to an observation that we caught a glimpse of earlier, but which is underdeveloped in Curran and Seaton's account: that the press, recorded music, film, radio, television, computing and the internet have all developed in very close proximity to the vastly larger telecommunications, electrical equipment manufacturing and banking firms since the mid-19th century (Miege 1989; Hesmondhalgh 2019). While it would take a book to comprehensively review this claim, I hope that a few highlights here will suffice to shed light on this point and its significance:

a. The press and news wire services developed in the shadows of telegraph companies the world over. This was central to the nationalisation of the telegraph industry in the UK, as noted earlier. The biggest source of censorship in the early 20th century, according to Walter Lippmann in *Liberty and the Press* (1920), was the cost of transmitting news on the wires, hence the push by reformers, with some success, in many countries for more affordable press rates.

b. In the US context, a Goliath versus emerging Goliath battle between the telegraph giants Western Union and AT&T in the late 1870s and early 1880s gave rise to the recorded music and filmed entertainment industries shortly thereafter (Danielian 1939, 92–110).

c. In the US and Canada, the 'Telephone Group' (AT&T and Western Electric) and the 'Radio Group' (GE, Westinghouse Electric and Manufacturing Company, RCA, United Fruit, Wireless Specialty Apparatus Company and Tropical Radio)—both of which had sprawling interests in nearly every industry that made up the infrastructure of 20th-century industrial capitalism *as well as the broadcasting and film industries*—engaged in round after round of battles throughout the 1920s that led to the fields being carved up between them. AT&T, for one, abandoned its fledgling Broadcasting Corporation of America as a result (Danielian 1939, 126–150).

d. Circumstances were similar in the UK, Germany, France and elsewhere. In each case, industrial manufacturing enterprises built up the technological side of radio broadcasting. In the UK, the big six electrical equipment manufacturing companies of the era—Marconi, Metropolitan-Vickers, British Thomson-Houston, the Radio Corporation of America, General Electric and Western Electric—created the British Broadcasting *Company* in 1922. Within four years, however, the British Government forced them out of the broadcasting business after refashioning the British Broadcasting *Company* into the public service, British Broadcasting *Corporation* (Briggs 1961/2000, 85–120, 297–35).

The lessons and legacy of *PWR*

As I hope to have conveyed, Curran and Seaton's *PWR* is a seminal text rich with enduring lessons for our own times, three of which I will briefly reprise by way of concluding this chapter.

Lesson #1: It is impossible to treat markets, politics and power as separate, walled-off spheres when studying the media. They are all intertwined and state intervention plays a key role in constituting both commercial media markets as well as public service organisations designed to address the reality that market failures and public goals are systemic in this domain. Consequently, public policy, subsidies and ownership are an indelible part of the 'free press' tradition in liberal capitalist democracies, not errant aberrations. In short, the media we have are fundamentally a function of politics, power and policy choices.

Lesson #2: The history of the modern media, and journalism in particular, in the shadow of the much larger sectors of telecommunications and the electrical equipment manufacturing industries, offers much insight into the relationship today between journalism and the media industries, on the one side, versus information technology giants such as Google, Amazon, Meta, Apple and Microsoft, on the other.

Lesson #3: Seeing the media industries as being totally subsumed by big tech might help secure favourable regulation and subsidies designed to uphold the viability of commercial journalism, but such views are 'sociologically and historically inaccurate and downplay similar long-standing tensions between the different sets of corporations and their varying interest' (Hesmondhalgh 2019, 472). Not only this, measures that we do need are likely to be obstructed by appeals to the myths of the free press that Curran and Seaton have done so much to bust while, even if one set of corporate interests—in this case publishers and media interests—does capture control of the policy agenda and prevail, the policy measures and subsidies adopted are likely to, simultaneously, lack legitimacy *and* fail to bring about the kind of internet, media systems and journalism that people and democracy need and deserve.

Ultimately, Curran and Seaton's *PWR* offers us the tools and imagination we need to recast old but recurring and urgent problems in a new light.

References

Briggs, A. A. 1961/2000. *The History of Broadcasting in the United Kingdom (vol. 1)*. Oxford University Press.

Curran, J. and Seaton, J. 2003. *Power Without Responsibility* (6th edition). Routledge.

Curran, J. and Seaton, J. 2018. *Power Without Responsibility* (8th edition). Routledge.

Danielian, Noobar R. 1939. *AT&T: The Story of Industrial Conquest.* Vanguard Press.

Hardt, H. 2001. *Social Theories of the Press*. Roman & Littlefield.

Hesmondhalgh, D. 2019. *The Cultural Industries* (4th edition). Sage Publications.

Horkheimer, M. and Adorno, T. 1947/2002. *The Dialectic of Enlightenment* (ed. Gunzelin Schmid Noerr). Stanford University Press.

John, R. 1998. *Spreading the News: The American Postal System from Franklin to Morse.* Harvard University Press.

Lippmann, W. 2018 [1920]. *Liberty and the News*. Routledge.

Miege, B. 1989. *The Capitalization of Cultural Production*. International General.

Pickard, V. 2022. Personal correspondence, February 23.

Sotiron, M. 1997. *From Politics to Profit: The Commercialization of Canadian Daily Newspapers, 1890–1920*. McGill-Queens University Press.

CHAPTER 14

Australia's Media Market Failure

Sally Young

One of the legacies of James Curran and Jean Seaton's *Power Without Responsibility* is that it encourages us to critically assess the role of the market. Australia is an unfortunate case study in this regard because it has had extremely high levels of concentration in commercial media ownership since the 1970s. This has had a harmful impact on public debate in Australia, but also beyond, because media owner Rupert Murdoch grew out of Australia's notoriously ruthless, media baron-yielding system and went on to achieve a level of global media dominance and political influence that has brought shame to Australians watching on as his outlets supported some of the most damaging philosophies, events and individuals of the 20th and 21st centuries.

Old media: Newspapers

In 1972, Rupert Murdoch was on the rise when he bought Sydney's *Daily Telegraph* from Australia's most notorious media baron-thug, Frank Packer. This left Australia with only three major newspaper owners at a time when newspapers still played a crucial role in communicating politics, policies and public affairs.

The three groups controlled more than 98% of all daily and Sunday newspapers sold in capital cities, and more than 90% of daily newspapers sold across Australia (Lawrence 1974, 2). Monopoly or duopoly was now the norm for daily papers in Australian capital cities. Sydney—which was considered the most turbulent and competitive market with four colourful owners battling it out in the early 1950s—was down to just two owners.

By 2011, an international study found that Australia had the most concentrated newspaper industry of any of the 30 countries studied, with the exceptions of China and Egypt with their state-dominated media (Noam 2016). One company—Murdoch's News Limited—controlled 60% of the market share of daily newspapers. In other words, his titles accounted for nearly 6 out of 10 daily sales in Australia (Papandrea and Tiffen 2016).

A lack of diversity in ownership meant a lack of political diversity in news and opinion that impoverished Australia's public debates and its political options. In 1928, Australia had 15 mainstream capital city newspapers. Fourteen of the 15 papers supported the conservative parties during the federal election (the other ran a non-committal election-eve editorial). Fast-forward 70 years to the 1998 federal election, and 10 of the 11 daily newspapers that ran election-eve editorials endorsed the conservative parties (again, the odd paper out was non-committal rather than endorsing an alternative party). Moving forward in time again, to the 2016 federal election, 12 out of 12 daily national/metropolitan newspapers supported the conservatives that year.

Although Australia had the first national labour government in the world (in 1904), the Labor Party rarely received support from the commercial newspapers and the lack of diversity extended beyond election endorsements and partisanship: it impacted the way political issues were reported and discussed, limiting options, viewpoints and potential remedies.

All of this became even more damaging when Australia's major newspaper owners took over the airwaves too. Conservative governments they had endorsed for office awarded licences to the major newspaper groups for the most important commercial radio and television stations. This gave the newspaper groups extraordinary cultural and political power.

Australian television

Australia's policymakers had only begun to seriously consider introducing television in the early 1950s. By then, Australia's already powerful newspaper groups had spent more than ten years studying television overseas, especially in the UK and the US. They knew exactly what they wanted to see in Australia—an American-style commercial television system that would allow newspaper publishers to become television broadcasters and reap the profits from commercial advertising. What they definitely did not want was a British-style system of public broadcasting that locked them out and instead gave a monopoly role to a taxpayer-funded broadcaster (in the UK, the BBC).

The newspaper groups' hopes and fears are recorded in their internal correspondence from this time, including documents held in the State Library's Fairfax Media Business Archive. A representative from Associated Newspapers, the company that owned the Sydney *Sun*, wrote from the US in 1954 to warn its chairman that 'we should undoubtedly press to get a [television] licence for ourselves' (Irish 1954). He noted that newspapers in New York were regretting they had not gone into television.

Some American newspaper groups were involved in commercial television but most were late or minor players and it was not enough to stop television's impact on their papers. The period between 1949 and 1959 was disastrous for American newspapers—217 daily newspapers disappeared and more than 1,200 American cities became one-paper towns (*US News and World Report* 1959).

Eric Kennedy, Associated Newspapers' chief executive officer, warned his bosses that Australian newspapers needed to get in early and 'control commercial television' (Kennedy 1953). The largest Australian newspaper groups were in an excellent position to achieve that control, not least because they were already radio broadcasters.

During the 1930s, metropolitan newspapers had been very successful in obtaining commercial radio licences from the conservative Lyons government. By 1954, newspapers owned—either wholly or partly—43 of the 106 commercial radio stations operating in Australia. The major newspaper groups now wanted to repeat that success and snare the first television licences. To achieve that, they used the power of their newspapers to shape public opinion and political decision-making, as well as their long experience in backroom lobbying and political campaigning.

In 1949, Labor's policy under leader Ben Chifley was to introduce a British-style public broadcasting system of television that would shut out the newspapers. His opponent, the conservative Liberal party leader, Robert Menzies, instead supported the newspapers' call for commercial television.

During the 1949 election, the major newspapers campaigned fiercely against Labor. After Menzies won, he announced a Royal Commission would make recommendations on television. It began in 1953 and was stacked to guarantee the newspapers a sympathetic hearing. Just to be safe, even before the Commission began its work, the Menzies government suddenly legislated for a dual system of public and commercial broadcasting. That settled the major issue at stake. Australia would have commercial stations as well as a public broadcaster, the ABC.

The Royal Commission's final report then recommended a television system that was almost a carbon-copy of the newspapers' proposals. Unlike several other countries, Australia's television licence holders would be able to own their own transmitters and face minimal content requirements or public service obligations. Now the race was on for the crucial first licences.

A clean sweep

Newspapers argued on their pages that they were the natural choice to be Australia's television pioneers. They played up concerns about foreign ownership which damaged the prospects of their main rivals, American cinema interests and foreign electrical manufacturers.

The newspapers also kept emphasising how expensive and financially risky it was going to be to start up a television station in Australia even though privately, they knew from the US, that although television *did* require an expensive capital investment, recovery was 'rapid', and first stations soon made 'phenomenal' profits (Stevenson 1951).

By the time commercial television licence applications were opened in 1955, the newspapers had frightened off potential competitors or else convinced them to join up with them. Across Australia's major cities, 10 of the first 11 commercial television licences were awarded to groups with a newspaper company as a major shareholder. The eleventh group had two newspapers as minor shareholders, and only five years later, it was owned by a separate newspaper company.

By 1960, it was a clean sweep. Newspaper groups were in control of all Australia's commercial television stations. As Labor's H.V. Evatt noted, no other country had allowed newspaper companies 'to become the sole pioneers in the field of commercial television' (Evatt 1956).

In Adelaide, Rupert Murdoch's News Limited, publisher of the *News*, was awarded one of the city's two television licences (NWS-9) in 1958. Despite all of the scaremongering about financial risk, Murdoch found, after a couple of lean years, that television could be highly profitable.

He would later buy his way into television in the larger markets of Melbourne and Sydney and sell the smaller NSW-9.

In Australia, before the mid-1980s, one company could own a daily metropolitan newspaper, a television station and radio station in the same city—and the big players did. Other countries put a stop to that. Even in the laissez-faire US, a 1940 'duopoly' rule prohibited ownership of a radio station and television station in the same market.

The television licences handed out in the 1950s had far-reaching consequences. One of these was the way television revenue helped transform Murdoch's News Limited from a small and insignificant Adelaide newspaper company in the 1950s into one of Australia's largest, and later, one of the world's largest media companies.

References

Evatt, H. V. 1956. *Hansard*, House of Representatives, 3 May.

Irish, R. A. 1954. Letter to John Butters, 19 July, FMBA, State Library of NSW, box 924, folder 68.

Kennedy, E. 1953. Report on television, 16 March, FMBA, State Library of NSW, box 924, folder 68.

Lawrence, J. 1974. A Government Newspaper. *Canberra Times*, 5 August.

Noam, E. 2016. Media Industries in International Comparison. In E. Noam (Ed.) *Who Owns the World's Media?: Media Concentration and Ownership Around the World*. Oxford University Press.

Papandrea, F. and Tiffen, R. 2016. Media Ownership and Concentration in Australia. In E. Noam (Ed.), *Who Owns the World's Media?: Media Concentration and Ownership Around the World*. Oxford University Press.

Stevenson, M. 1951. Report, February, FMBA, State Library of NSW, box 924, folder 68.

US News and World Report 1959. Why Newspapers are Having Trouble. 16 January.

Media Reform: Democratic Choices

CHAPTER 15

Why Has Media Reform Failed?

Leo Watkins

Over four years on from Labour's 2019 electoral defeat, the brief period in which the party leadership appeared open to radically reforming the media is now clearly over. One of the strongest bases of opposition to the Corbyn project was the national press which, in the UK, is heavily dominated by the right. Even nominally left-of-centre titles like the *Guardian* and *Daily Mirror* were, at most, lukewarm in their support and tended to be actively hostile.

Those of us who have campaigned for progressive media reform spend most of our energy assembling the case for reform and discussing radical policy ideas. We spend relatively little time explaining why past efforts to achieve even moderate, progressive reform—let alone anything radical—have so often failed. This chapter suggests an answer to that question by way of an engagement with the chapter of *Power Without Responsibility* entitled 'Industrial folklore and press reform'.

In that chapter, Curran and Seaton outline the postwar history of progressive attempts to reform the UK press as a series of four reform 'moments'. First, a 'public service moment' under the Attlee government in the 1940s, whose chief advocate was the National Union of Journalists and whose goal was the professionalisation of newspaper journalism. Second, a 'radical Keynesian moment' in the 1960s, whose goals were to counteract growing economic concentration and sustain a diversity of perspectives in the press. Third, a 'democratising moment' in the 1970s, led by press and broadcasting unions and workers, whose goals were the acquisition of workers' control in media industries and a reduction in the power of media owners. After a long gap, the fourth was a 'moment of outrage' in 2011 created by the phone hacking scandal, which led to the Leveson Inquiry. Here, the campaigners' goal was quite modest: to establish a new regime of press self-regulation backed up by a monitoring regime established by legislation and accountable to Parliament. The chapter's correct verdict is that each of these moments ended in failure.

Why was reform defeated each time? There are two strands to *Power Without Responsibility*'s explanation. The first is that the press was 'a powerful and determined institution that was unashamedly self-serving', able to exploit Westminster political connections and present a united front against reform despite internal political differences. Centrist and centre-left newspapers are ideologically 'led' by right-wing titles who have deployed a self-serving conception of press freedom, 'a creed of righteous libertarianism' (Curran and Seaton 2018, 475).

The press equates the exemption of newspaper companies and their owners from any industry-specific regulation imposed *or even merely monitored at arm's length* by Parliament with protecting 'the freedom of the press', and portrays any such regulation as 'state censorship'. Underlying this is the idea that the freedom of newspaper owners to maximise profit without regulation is in the interest of society as a whole— even when that involves printing falsehoods, violating basic ethical and professional standards, and undermining public trust in the media. This view denies that threats to media freedom can originate outside the state from sources whose influence state regulation or subsidy can counteract, such as dependence on advertising revenue or the power of private media owners. The book challenges this 'righteous libertarianism' (Curran and Seaton 2018, 181) by pointing to the effects of 'market censorship' on the newspaper industry caused by its dependence on advertising revenue and by the rising capital requirements of industrialised newspaper publishing. These precluded all but the wealthiest from owning and running private, mass-market news media, and built a pervasive pro-capitalist bias into the newspaper market that obviated the need for state censorship in late 19th-century Britain. This strand of the book's explanation is compelling.

The second strand of the book's explanation is an argument that in the 1945–79 period there was 'little pressure for press reform' and then from 1979 onwards 'little opportunity' because politicians 'lost power' over the past 35 years when the press has become too powerful for them to take on (Curran and Seaton 2018, 475–6). But neither claim is true, as the book's own history shows.

First, there *was* pressure for reform, primarily from organised labour in the newspaper industry. For example, the Labour cabinet established the 1947 Royal Commission on the press as a concession to the National Union of Journalists. The phrase 'little pressure' hints at the real issue: that the Labour leadership had to be externally 'pressured' to act because it did not itself see the need to do anything. The NUJ remained a consistent advocate of professionalising measures. In the 1970s, some workers in the industry became radicalised and started developing an agenda for workers' control. In fact, Raymond Williams and other New Left intellectuals had begun to develop an agenda for the democratisation of media and communications back in the late 1950s and early 1960s but senior Labour politicians, including Harold Wilson, prevented these from becoming Labour policy (*New Left Review* 1961).

Second, the claim that there was 'little opportunity' after 1979 seems dubious. The book argues that political leaders ceased to be in charge of effective party machines, evidenced by falling party membership, and that they enjoyed diminished 'cultural capital' and prestige, evidenced by the decline of strong party identification, declining voter turnout and increasing public distrust of politicians.

Against this it must first be noted that, constitutionally speaking, the 'opportunity' to tackle the press did not decline. Under the UK's unwritten constitution, a simple Commons majority is all a government requires to legislate to regulate or reform the press. Since 1979 there has been, on average, a governing majority of 91 seats, compared to 55 in the years from 1945 to 1979. The 2011 phone-hacking scandal presented politicians with an unrivalled opportunity to reform the press, and all parties professed themselves committed to doing so. But the opportunity was squandered and is now definitively past. Only in one sense did the 'opportunity' really decline in this period: organised labour, the main advocate of reform and professionalisation within the industry, was smashed in the 1980s—and the Thatcher government actively aided employers in doing so, which suggests that for that government at least, what was lacking was less opportunity than motive.

The key change is really one of *increased party competition for media support* because of a political convergence between the two main parties on neoliberal terrain, as deindustrialisation and the defeat of organised labour—both aims of Thatcher government policy—combined with repeated electoral defeats led Labour to abandon postwar social democracy and accept the Thatcherite settlement. This included extremely restrictive trade union laws that helped preclude a comeback of trade union power in the press. For New Labour, it was above all the pursuit of an accommodation with established media power that precluded any serious interest in progressive media reform.

This was novel in the history of the Labour Party and provided the Conservatives with much more serious competition for the support of right-wing media owners—Rupert Murdoch in particular—than it had ever faced before. It was this political convergence that really explains the symptoms of political decay the book cites in evidence. The defeat and decline of organised labour led to a decline in working-class politicisation and electoral mobilisation. The reduced political stakes of elections in which the two parties offered extremely similar policy prospectuses reduced the reasons to be a party member or cast a vote. The lack of a strong, clear political divide between parties reduced the meaning or purpose of strong partisan affiliation.

What really explains the defeat of press reform? The answer lies in the fact that neither of Britain's two main parties has ever seriously desired to reform the press, but for fundamentally different reasons. The Conservative Party has historically had little desire to reform the press because the right-wing papers which dominate it use their power broadly to the long-term benefit of the political right. The lack of press standards regulation or mechanisms for redress means there are few constraints on the press making propaganda, monstering and intimidating its most dangerous political opponents—usually those of the Conservatives too—and fostering moral panics or assisting in the discursive and media construction of dangerous 'others'. In short, the Conservatives are more often the beneficiaries than the losers from the press's unregulated freedom to violate basic journalistic standards. From the Zinoviev letter in the 1920s to the 'loony left' in the 1980s and the vilification of Corbyn in the 2010s, press standards have been abandoned repeatedly in the interests of the Conservatives and the broader right.

The more interesting question is why has Labour shown such a long-standing lack of desire to reform the press? Three reasons can be suggested.

First, the press is perceived as 'too powerful to take on' by Labour's leaders. This was the reason given by, for example, Tony Blair in his evidence to the Leveson Inquiry. But this can't be the whole story: if successive Labour leaders had truly been committed to taking on the press, and only deterred from doing so by a pragmatic realism about capitalist press power, their reaction ought to have been to energetically support the development of party and movement media that could help counteract the influence of the capitalist press. Yet at no time in Labour's history has the party's leadership made this a priority.

Second, Labour leaders have basically accepted the definition of 'freedom of the press' as immunity from sectoral regulation and opposition to subsidies—the 'creed of righteous libertarianism'. That is to say, they have accepted a *capitalist* definition of press freedom as the unregulated power of press owners. Here, *PWR* exhibits what Labour has long been missing: a thoroughgoing critique of the market as an *alternative* mechanism for regulating and indeed often censoring media production—one that systematically skews the media to the right. But this theoretical incapacity is part of the broader one the New Left called 'Labourism': the prevailing ideology held by those at the top of the Labour Party that seeks an accommodation with, rather than the transcendence of, capitalism.

Worse, Labour's leaders have not only uncritically accepted a capitalist definition of press freedom, they have also consistently shown a failure to recognise the crucial politico-strategic importance of the media terrain at all—a failure of which the Conservatives cannot be accused. It is a striking fact, shown by Curran and Seaton, that virtually every major instance of British media policymaking in the 20th and 21st centuries has been by Conservative governments: the creation of the BBC, ITV, Channel 4 and Channel 5; the launch of satellite broadcasting; three of the five major inquiries into the press (the two launched under Labour went nowhere). The single exception is the 2003 Communications Act, whose basic thrust was to continue Thatcherite deregulation and install a regulator oriented towards social market goals. The Labour leadership's attempt to deregulate media ownership laws was only reversed by a backbench rebellion of Labour peers led by the film producer David Puttnam. It is telling that the title of *Power Without Responsibility* comes from a speech strongly criticising the press made by a Conservative and not a Labour leader.

Third, the internal position of the right wing of the Labour Party, which has held the party's parliamentary leadership for most of the party's history, is fundamental. The Labour right's leading position has at times been challenged by the left, often in the immediate aftermath of a period in office during which a Labour government has, in Ralph Miliband's words, 'moved from being agents of reform to agents of conservative retrenchment', ending in an electoral debacle (Miliband 1983, 292). Outside state office, the Labour leadership is potentially vulnerable to challenge through the party's main democratic mechanisms, limited though these may be: election of the leader, candidate selections, conference votes and the election of National Executive Committee members (though only 9 out of 39 are directly elected by party members).

In the inner-party struggle for control, the party right has always played the trump card that, however radical the party's members and supporters may want its programme to be, a radical programme is unable to provide the basis for electoral victory. Only a programme of moderate, credible, electable policies—those of the party right—will apparently lead to such victory. It is this claim to a monopoly on pragmatic political realism, along with technical competence, on which the party's right wing has consistently based its claim to lead. In fighting off challenges to its leadership by the party left, the media has at times proven *a key ally of the party right*: stigmatising and delegitimising the party left, constructing a 'cross-party' agreement to which the Conservatives are only too happy to assent that Labour risks becoming 'too extreme' if led from the left, and alternately attacking and mocking attempts by the party to win office on a more radical programme.

Of course, what this entails is that the party right does not necessarily object to, or find especially problematic, a configuration of economic, political and media power that makes it extremely hard for the Labour Party to win general elections on a platform outside the bounds of what those who hold such power define as acceptable or 'credible'. And that much better explains the consistent absence of desire on the part of Labour's leaders to take on the undeniably major strategic challenge of progressive press reform.

In conclusion, it is important to recognise that the broader British left, and even at times parts of the Labour Party itself, have consistently generated a wealth of ideas for progressive media reform. But these have not usually found their way into official party policy, and never into actual legislation (*New Left Review* 1961). It is this disconnect, above all, on which explanations of the failure of progressive media reform efforts must centre.

Ralph Miliband (1983, 292) argued that Labourism 'readily accepted the political system that was in existence when the labour movement assumed definite shape in the second half of the nineteenth century'. Curran and Seaton's account of 19th-century press history suggests a possible reason why this occurred: the decline of the radical press as an agent of oppositional class formation and the rise of a commercial press that instead promoted class accommodation. Here we need an internationally comparative theory of the role played in class formation by different national presses: to investigate what Gramsci (1995, 155) once called 'the material organisation intended to maintain, defend and develop the theoretical or ideological "front"', as it was shaped by different national class structures and by uneven and combined capitalist development.

References

Curran, J. and Seaton, J. 2018. *Power Without Responsibility: Press, Broadcasting and Internet in Britain*. 8th edition. Routledge.

Gramsci, A. 1995. *Further Selections from The Prison Notebooks*. Edited and translated by Derek Boothman. Lawrence and Wishart.

Miliband, R. 1983. Socialist Advance in Britain. In R. Miliband 2015, *Class War Conservatism and Other Essays*. Verso.

New Left Review 1961. Missing Signposts. *New Left Review*, I/12, 9–10.

CHAPTER 16

A *Manifesto for a People's Media*: A Response to *Power Without Responsibility*

Natalie Fenton

Power Without Responsibility (Curran and Seaton 2018) has been a foundational text and normative framework for the field. It tells a fascinating story that continues to resonate today and relates a press and broadcasting history that helps us to understand the state of our mediated world in the UK and beyond.

In the latest 2018 edition, we learn about the fourth estate myth in relation to the majority of the mainstream press in the UK, press-politician entanglement, commercial imperatives, billionaire moguls and the myth of market democracy. We read about how the press has performed the role of the neo-liberal establishment; how it has consistently scorned the working class and published misogynistic and xenophobic storylines that blame immigrants for decreasing living standards; how it favours a pro-law and order narrative to keep the unruly poor in check as well as communists, loony lefties and terrorists (often one and the same); and how it has contributed to the development of an elite neoliberal political culture.

On broadcasting, we learn about consistent government attacks on the BBC and its complex relationship to the British state; the dominance of managerialism and the commercial interests of multinational empires who see the BBC as inconvenient competition. It addresses the issues of accountability, the problems with maintaining public values, independence, and the debate between 'choice' and public service. In relation to the internet, we read how a logic of profit and power remains but also holds possibilities with the argument made that commercialism will prevail online unless there is a countervailing force.

The final section on media politics crucially addresses issues of media reform. If we agree that major media outlets and digital intermediaries are captured by global capitalism to the detriment of democracy then what can we do about it? What is the response of society when the ability to speak truth to power is restricted by corporate logic? How do we react when the possibility of an independent check on the activities of political and corporate elites is limited by their entanglement? How can we reclaim concepts like 'freedom' and 'pluralism' that have traditionally served radical democratic agendas but are now corrupted and used to prop up capital? How do you build a movement and a media based on a wholly different, democratic approach to communication? Although *PWR* doesn't quite put the argument in these terms, much of the discussion within it leads us to this point and it is where the work of the Media Reform Coalition and our *Manifesto for a People's Media: Creating a Media Commons* takes off (Media Reform Coalition 2021).

The manifesto begins from the position that we need to understand the capitalist social system as a totality. It is clear that the UK and the wider world are facing multiple, interconnected global crises including huge and growing inequality; the health and economic fallout of the pandemic; growing democratic deficits and the rise of the far right around the globe; Russia's invasion of Ukraine, Israel's assault on Gaza and other ongoing wars around the world; alongside catastrophic climate change and ecological collapse. Woven through all of these crises is a loss of trust in institutions, including the institutions which are meant to inform and educate us about the world—our media. Trust in media in the UK is at a record low—69% believe the media is failing to be objective and non-partisan (Edelman 2021, 36). The media landscape is dominated by huge, unaccountable corporations. Digital platforms are the biggest monopolies the world has ever seen, while 90% of the UK's daily national newspaper market is owned by just three companies (Media Reform Coalition 2023, 2). Despite an abundance of content, there are 'worrying gaps and deficits in news produced for and in local communities' with approximately 23% of the UK population living in either a newspaper 'desert' or 'drought' (ibid., 17).

Underlying many of these problems is the fact that in the press world at least, the economic model of funding through advertising is failing. Research from across the globe shows the commercial model is increasingly unable to produce news and cultural content in the public interest, and there is an urgent need for a different approach to funding our media including large-scale investment from governments to prevent it being swallowed up by commercialism or disappearing altogether.

Dealing with the huge challenges that we face means having a media system oriented towards the public interest, rather than the interests of politicians, wealthy owners or powerful businesses. It means having a system which is able to harness the huge potential of digital technologies and data for the public good, rather than seeing them captured for private benefit. Our public service media—institutions like the BBC and Channel 4—have a crucial role to play, and need to be strengthened and transformed for the digital age. But this transformation can't be confined to those institutions. It needs a far more wide-ranging transition: the revitalisation of existing public media, as part of the creation of what we call a 'media commons'.

Creating a media commons is not just about finding alternative approaches to and policies for media but also developing an alternative politics that begins from a concern with the problems a capitalist economy has left us with: burgeoning inequality, precarity and poverty; global warming and the biospheric damage from a dominant economic system predicated on endless consumption and growth that concentrates economic and political power in the hands of the few.

To change this direction of travel requires political and economic alternatives that are just and inclusive, ecologically wise and socially regenerative shifting economic and political power back to communities and public democratic institutions. In other words, conceiving of a mediated society that supports a newly imagined democratic political economy means conceiving of a world not simply post-Covid but post-capitalism.

The *Manifesto for a People's Media* attempts to claim a transformative media politics through a focus on the media as public goods that are independent, accountable, democratic and for everyone, through public forms of ownership, collective forms of governance and social control of finance: the commons as an alternative to capitalism rather than the commons as a substitute for the welfare state or even public service broadcasting. A commons is a collective resource sustained through the active participation of those who rely on it. Organisations within the media commons would be funded by significant new public investment, recognising that the commercial model of media leads to unaccountable monopolies and exacerbates inequalities and cannot provide the journalistic and cultural content that we need. Advocating for a media commons also means refusing ever-increasing levels of extraction, production and consumption promulgated by media and tech companies.

A media commons in the UK would include a people's BBC and Channel 4, transformed to become far more devolved and participatory. Rather than just interacting with them as passive audiences, people would help make decisions about how they are run—whether that involves electing decision-makers to represent them, being part of participatory commissioning or sitting on a panel to oversee coverage of controversial issues. Because of this, they would be widely trusted and embedded in people's lives. Such a vision would also include a British Digital Cooperative to develop a national-scale digital infrastructure and an independent media commons—a thriving ecology of participatory newsrooms, community radio stations, digital innovators and cultural producers, supported by democratically controlled public resources to tell the stories of all the UK's communities. New funding of around £1 billion a year would be distributed through a network of national and regional Media Councils using participatory methods (drawing on learning from participatory budgeting and grant-making) to support news journalism, cultural content and digital innovation.

This is a bold vision because it is trying to suggest a media commons not just in one area or organisation but throughout the entire UK, across all media sectors, by establishing structures that are inclusively managed, decentralised and participatory. It is a vision that speaks to the digressions, eviscerations and amputations of media as a public good that *Power Without Responsibility* so eruditely describes. This is a vision that seeks to enable, support and sustain forms of media and tech ownership that are counter to capitalist enterprise, not-for-profit and fully independent of commercial pressures and government preferences, organised cooperatively and democratically and are responsive to the needs of the communities they serve rather than operating at the behest of the market.

Through proposing a media commons, the *Manifesto for a People's Media* recognises that we need systemic change and introduces a new logic of de-commodification of the social commons where our media and tech institutions can be reclaimed for the public good. It is one response to the problems that *PWR* has been highlighting for over 40 years. Without alternative visions, without setting out the necessity for radical reforms, without understanding our media and tech systems as part of the totality of a capitalist social and political economic system, there will be many more editions of *PWR* before any meaningful media reform takes place that can address the challenges it poses.

References

Edelman 2021. *Edelman Trust Barometer: Trust in the UK Report.* Available at: https://www.edelman.co.uk/edelman-trust-barometer-2021-uk-findings

Media Reform Coalition 2021. *Manifesto for a People's Media.* Media Reform Coalition. Available at: https://www.mediareform.org.uk/get-involved/manifesto-for-a-peoples-media

Media Reform Coalition 2023. *Who Owns the UK Media?* Media Reform Coalition. Available at: https://www.mediareform.org.uk/wp-content/uploads/2023/10/Who-Owns-the-UK-Media-2023.pdf

CHAPTER 17

Against Market Censorship: A Call for Democratising Journalism

Victor Pickard

Journalism and capitalism have always been in tension. Pegging news media so directly to market relationships has led to predictable problems, from racial and class-based red-lining to ever-expanding news deserts to incentivising the production of low-quality information. Yet, media scholarship typically has taken the commercial system for granted, with precious few works systematically interrogating it. James Curran and Jean Seaton's classic *Power Without Responsibility* belongs to this special canon.

Their foundational book—first published in 1981 but timelier now than ever—denaturalises the media's systemic characteristics and provides us with the necessary tools to critically analyse political economic relationships from historical, normative and structural perspectives.

In their magisterial review of British media history, Curran and Seaton cut against popular mythologies that see the press becoming increasingly independent and pluralistic over time. The book shows that, contrary to the Whiggish historical account of steady progress toward greater press freedoms and heroic struggles against censorship, the shift to advertising—and a more market-driven system in general—in fact introduced *greater* levels of censorship in the press.

Curran and Seaton also demonstrate that the structural shift towards commercialisation was particularly devastating for what had been a vibrant radical press. Increasing market dependence created a media landscape that was easily dominated by oligarchs who constricted the views and voices within the press, while naturalising right-wing perspectives.

A similar historical pattern played out in the US, where the structural transformation was quite severe. As the press became increasingly commercialised and depoliticised in the late 1800s, the shifting political economy completely altered newspaper content and publishers' relationship to audiences (Pickard 2020; Baldasty 1992). The audience came to be seen less as engaged *citizens* of a polity and more as passive *consumers* whose attention advertisers sought to capture, and publishers used as bait for greater revenues.

This focus on what happens to the press as it increasingly commercialises over time—and the implications of that structural shift for democracy—is just one of many key lessons that emerge from Curran and Seaton's painstaking historical research. Their analysis points to important relationships between the market, the press, and democracy—especially one key concept that they mention several times but stands to be further developed: market censorship.

Exposing market censorship

Market censorship can be understood as the process of systemic omissions and emphases that predictably manifest in a heavily commercialised press. Several scholars have since picked up on this theme—it has been central to developing critical inquiries in my own work (e.g. Pickard 2020)—but this structural pathology warrants further attention and development. It also calls for a vibrant discussion as to how we can best contest it.

Typically, the word 'censorship' evokes fears of oppressive governments or perhaps corporate media policing the parameters of acceptable discourse and narrowing the range of political opinion. Of course, such abuses do happen and are legitimate concerns. However, a deeper, more systemic, form of censorship corrupts our media institutions as they become overly commercialised and more closely intertwined with capitalist imperatives.

This subtle—but no less malignant—sorting process that arises as a byproduct of toxic commercialism adheres to a set of values that systematically privilege entertainment over information and consistently marginalise progressive arguments and issues. Resulting in a corrupted public sphere and an impoverished political imaginary, this capitalist logic shapes and warps much of our news and information. It creates patterns of omission and emphasis—where some voices and views are elevated and others stifled according to commercial values, profit accumulation and corporate power.

The idea of market censorship has received only sporadic attention in media scholarship over the years. Sue Curry Jansen (2010) offers what might be the best definition: 'Market censorship points to practices that routinely filter or restrict the production and distribution of selected ideas, perspectives, genres or cultural forms within mainstream media... based upon their anticipated profits and/or support for corporate values and consumerism' (2010, 13).

Similarly, C. Edwin Baker observed that such recurring patterns trace back to the negative impact of advertising which, he notes, acts as the 'most consistent and the most pernicious "censors" of media content' (1994, 3). For their part, Herman and Chomsky (1988) indicted advertising and the dependence on commercial imperatives as one of the chief 'filters' in their 'propaganda model'.

This commercial censoring of our news and information must be confronted to build structural alternatives to the corporate, heavily commercialised, and lightly regulated media system in the US—and to only a slightly lesser degree in the UK. As activists, we need to connect these dots and draw explicit linkages between a commercial media system's structural characteristics and the various deficits and harms that manifest in media content. Ultimately, we should ask: what does this mean for media reform?

A new media reform agenda

Curran and Seaton's work holds important lessons for setting a new media reform agenda. First, they underscore the centrality of media—and the impediments that a market-driven media system pose—for any activist project. Former Federal Communications Commissioner Nicholas Johnson famously argued that whatever your first political priority is your second should be media reform—otherwise you will not make progress on your first issue. A market-driven media system will almost always champion the status quo, which means that working toward social change should include not just de-commercialising but also, as important, *democratising* our media.

This argument seems obvious enough, but we should place an even finer point on it to be crystal clear: a market-dependent media system is incompatible with democratic objectives. Ultimately, we should treat news and information as public services that should never be left entirely to the mercy of capitalist logics. We therefore must build systemic and sustainable alternatives to anti-democratic commercial models.

In getting there, however, we must also be clear in our language and in our framing. Too rarely do we directly indict capitalism for driving these market values that debase and destroy actual journalism. Since structural critiques of capitalism have been beaten out of the discourse over the years, we often miss the forest for the trees and fail to understand the systemic biases at work. We must be clear that journalism and capitalism were always an ill-conceived match, and it is beyond time to sever this unholy union. In place of the dying commercial model, we need public, independent and democratic models. Gradually we should remove journalism from the market altogether.

This process could take many forms and look different in different national contexts, some more ambitiously utopian than others. UK media reform activists have provided a useful blueprint for radically restructuring and democratising commercial media—as well as establishment public service broadcasting such as the BBC (Fenton et al. 2020). For the American context, I have called for building 'public media centers' in every community that are federally guaranteed but locally governed (Pickard 2021; Pickard 2023). However, we also must further internationalise media reform coalitions beyond Anglo-American circles to include other regions around the world, especially in the global South.

The underlying principles of these public models, regardless of national context, should be universal. They should translate to mean the collective ownership of the means of media production so that newsrooms are owned and controlled by communities and by journalists themselves. It means treating journalism as a public service devoted to democracy, not a commodity devoted to generating profit for a small group of owners and investors. And it means always striving for universal service where all members of society have access to a baseline level of news and information, but who also are empowered to tell their own stories and make their own media.

In striving for these radical goals, upon which so much depends, we can be inspired by the paths blazed by Curran and Seaton. Consistently, they have called out the hazards posed by extreme commercialism and monopoly power in our news media. They have helped cultivate our understanding about the nuanced role of public broadcasting in a democratic society, as well as the role of policy in shaping media systems. And they have remained steadfast in their defence of core democratic principles. Their book, *Power Without Responsibility*, is a foundational text for thinking through these problems and confronting them: a noble and necessary struggle, and one incumbent upon us all to continue.

References

Baker, C. E. 1994. *Advertising and a Democratic Press*. Princeton University Press.

Baldasty, G. 1992. *The Commercialization of News in the Nineteenth Century*. University of Wisconsin Press.

Curran, J. and Seaton J. 2018. *Power Without Responsibility*, 8th edition. Routledge.

Fenton, N., Freedman, D., Schlosberg, J., and Dencik, L. 2020. *The Media Manifesto*. Polity Press.

Herman, E. and Chomsky, N. 1988. *Manufacturing Consent: The Political Economy of the Mass Media*. Pantheon Books.

Jansen, S. C. 2010. Ambiguities and Imperatives of Market Censorship: The Brief History of a Critical Concept. *Westminster Papers in Communication and Culture*, 7(2).

Pickard, V. 2020. *Democracy Without Journalism? Confronting the Misinformation Society*. Oxford University Press.

Pickard, V. 2021. From the Ashes: Imagining a Post-Commercial Future for Media. *The Political Economy of Communication*, 9(1), 79–83.

Pickard, V. 2023. Another Media System is Possible: Ripping Open the Overton Window from Platforms to Public Broadcasting. *Javnost: The Public*, 30 (2), 284–297.

CHAPTER 18

Paradise Lost: Why We Need a Public Service Internet and How it Could Save Our Democracy

Klaus Unterberger

The wars in Gaza and Ukraine, severe societal fragmentation following the Covid-19 pandemic, populistic and nationalistic regimes endangering independence of media: if we look at today's scenarios of crisis, there is no doubt that democracy is at stake. The loss of security and rising social tensions are shattering the comfort zone of postwar Europe and its assurance of never-ending economic growth creating the basis for an expanding, blooming civil society. The atmosphere and mindset of the 'golden age' of the 'boomer' generation have been replaced with massive insecurity and fear, causing alarming distrust in institutions, media and representative democracy.

In fact, it is even worse: simultaneous climate and social crisis work like binary agents of warfare, creating unexpected and most of all disruptive consequences destroying traditional structures and mindsets. This momentum, a *Zeitenwende*, as the German Chancellor Olaf Scholz defines it, a *turning point* in history may have dramatic consequences including the emergence of a battlefield in Europe, a new Cold War, the rise of the extreme right, including neo-Nazis and fascists out on the street, social riots, imploding democracies and a collapsing climate. What seemed to be dystopian yesterday is a realistic perspective today and might become a historic rollback for society framed by catastrophic scenarios. It is paradise lost where the narratives have changed significantly: from progress to regression and from hope to fear.

If we look at the internet, there is the same story. Didn't we expect a bright new future, with information available for everyone? A new dimension of diversity? A new and effective toolkit for civic participation leading towards a new empowered democracy? Instead, what we got is quite different: a digital world owned by a handful of companies and CEO's creating their own playing field beyond public interest and control. Instead of democracy for all, we are facing a new feudalism with a handful of data barons, more or less friendly or weird, more or less liberal or autocratic, more or less in line with democracy, but all of them significantly unaccountable to the public. The era of an actor (or a weirdo) as POTUS might become an overture of a global decline of democracy: what if Mark Zuckerberg, Peter Thiel or Elon Musk decide to run for president? After all they have the money, the power and, most of all, they are already connected with their potential voters, addressing them individually as consumers, no longer as citizens.

Even if we don't take scenarios like that into account: What makes us believe that the current status of quality media is built in stone and that free, independent, accountable and trusted media will prevail? Who or what guarantees that democracy will *not* fail?

Despite all the great opportunities digital technologies have offered society and individuals, the hopes and expectations of a free and democratic internet are broken. Digital giants, led by Apple, Alphabet/Google, Microsoft, Amazon, Alibaba, Meta/Facebook and Tencent, have acquired unparalleled economic, political and cultural power. They undermine the indispensable resources of trusted information, in-depth analysis, rational debate and diversity of representation that allow us to fully understand the challenges we face. They have created a communication landscape dominated by surveillance, advertising, fake news, hate speech, conspiracy theories and the algorithmic allocation of users to commercial and political content tailored to their expressed tastes and opinions. As currently organised, the internet separates and divides instead of creating common spaces for negotiating difference and disagreement. In fact, the dominant forms and uses of digital technologies and the internet endanger democracy itself.

The way forward

Despite all dystopian scenarios and perspectives, there is good news in that useful alternatives for change are already at hand. As a consequence of the devastation of World War II and the barbaric regime of the Nazis and its mass manipulating propaganda, democratic societies have established Public Service Media (PSM), defined, commissioned, contracted by the public, funded by the public and controlled by the public. We all know that its current state is far from perfect. There is plenty of evidence of serious challenges and deficits. Having worked for PSM more than 40 years myself, I can tell. However, there is no better way to fulfil a democratic remit in communications than a public service media that focus not on commercial interest but on social cohesion. It would be a serious mistake not to use the existing infrastructure of Public Service Media for the creation of a Public Service Internet.

This is why an international group of scientists and media experts recently published a Manifesto for a Public Service Internet (Fuchs and Unterberger 2021).[1] It is globally spread and already supported by more than 1,200 academics, scientists and media experts worldwide, including Jürgen Habermas and Noam Chomsky. Its vision defines specific quality criteria:

- The Public Service Internet is based on existing networks, infrastructure and logistics, as well as competence and experience of Public Service Media. It takes the societal consensus of the public service remit and applies it to the digital age. It creates strong cooperation with civil society, individual media users, citizens, and creative, cultural and educational sectors.
- Public Service Internet platforms are ideally operated as international networks curated by Public Service Media organisations. Public Service Internet platforms cooperate with public organisations (universities, museums, libraries, etc.), civil society, civic and community media, artists, digital commons projects, platform cooperatives and a wide range of quality media. In fact, it creates a public-civic partnership using societal resources. Public Service Media organisations, together with public interest organisations, create open, public online spaces, which form the Public Service Internet.
- The Public Service Internet will have to defend its independence to ensure that editorial and creative decisions are separate from governmental and business interests. Safeguarding Public Service Internet's role as a trusted and independent source of information and analysis as well as a responsible mediator, curator and moderator of independently produced and user-generated content requires transparent procedures of

accountability. Such procedures need to be based on clear ethical principles of governance, editorial guidelines and quality control.

- At a safe distance from corporate and political power, it can produce critical investigative journalism and high-quality programmes that educate, inform and entertain in ways that reflect the affordances of the digital age and the diversity of society. It can engage citizens in new forms of communication that build on the experiences, structures and content of the Public Service Broadcast model and use the creative potential of digital content production through user participation. Public Service Internet's remit will therefore be to create a new Digital Public Service.

- Reflecting the needs of the public and supporting citizenship, Public Service Media provide the ideal foundation to create and house a new Public Service Search Engine and Platform, directing users to the full range of freely available relevant material produced and curated by public educational and cultural institutions.

- Consequently, data privacy is a core aspect of the Public Service Internet. It provides role model practices of data processing. Public Service Internet software is a common good that can be reused for non-commercial purposes. On Public Service Internet platforms, users can manage their data, and download and re-use their self-curated data on other platforms. The digital giants store every click and every online move in order to monitor and monetise behaviour. Public Service Internet platforms minimise and decentralise data storage and have no need to monetise and monitor internet use. Public Service Internet platforms experiment with new forms of content licensing that advance the cultural and digital commons for not-for-profit and non-commercial purposes.

- The Public Service Internet's algorithms are publicly controlled. Such algorithms are open source and transparent. They are programmed in ways that advance the Digital Public Service remit. Public service algorithms are produced by the public and for the public. They help organise the platforms, formats and content of the Public Service Internet by making recommendations and suggestions based on transparent procedures, without advertising, commerce and surveillance. Public service algorithms reflect the diversity of the public and advance accessibility, fairness and inclusivity.

- The Public Service Internet will be a driver of change. Its news and entertainment provision will pay particular attention to developing innovative styles of media production that highlight, explain and contextualise issues with far-reaching social implications and their possible consequences. Public Service Internet will build on its proven strengths to produce innovative programmes and online content that support children's educational development, speak to the full range of young people's interests and concerns, and provide comprehensive resources for life-long adult learning. In the digital future, as in the past, entertainment, drama and sport will remain central aspects of public cultural expression and social solidarity. Public Service Internet will play a central role in maximising the social value of public cultural resources.

- The Public Service Internet must provide new opportunities for participation to safeguard diversity, inclusion and democracy. Civil society supports a rich variety of self-organised, collaborative, activity-producing, collective resources, from community choirs to groups protecting wildlife habitats or those campaigning for disadvantaged groups using new forms of digital action, from creating open source software to contributing to citizen science projects. Public Service Internet will utilise the full range of voluntary engagement and develop new forms of popular participation in key areas such as the production of programmes and the creation of Public Service Internet resources.

- A public and commons-based internet is possible—an internet on which people share, communicate, decide, discuss, play, create, criticise, network, collaborate, find, maintain and build friendships, fall in love, entertain themselves and each other, and educate themselves as common activity without corporate mediation.

The *Manifesto*, described here, is a vision, a wake-up call. Public communication is more than business; it is a public purpose. More than ever, democratic societies need media and a public sphere that reflects the needs of their citizens. At the same time, the *Manifesto* is a call for action. It is a call to save and advance democratic communication by renewing Public Service Media and creating a Public Service Internet: an internet of the public, by and for the public; an internet that advances instead of threatens democracy and the public sphere, that provides a new and dynamic shared space for connection, exchange and collaboration; an internet enhancing the public sphere, supporting active citizenship and young creatives who will build the cultural industries of tomorrow, and foster social cohesion.

There are good reasons why we cannot accept the dominance of the digital giants, why we cannot allow hidden algorithmic structures to exploit our private sphere and manipulate us. Being confronted with an authoritarian Russian regime that misuses media for propaganda, we should be more than ever convinced that we need a public sphere that is free of governmental oppression as well as business dominance. In fact, it is still the vision of free and independent media acting as the 'Fourth Estate' of democracy, controlling government, political as well as business interests, to safeguard the fundamental basis of our free and democratic societies. This is why we need a new internet that serves the public, supports citizenship and creates stakeholder, not shareholder, value.

Note

1 You can sign the Manifesto at http://bit.ly/signPSManifesto

Reference

Fuchs, C. and Unterberger, K. (Eds.) 2021. *The Public Service Media and Public Service Internet Manifesto*. University of Westminster Press. Available at: https://www.uwestminsterpress.co.uk/site/books/e/10.16997/book60/

Part IV

Public Interest: A Historical and Contemporary Analysis

CHAPTER 19

Speaking Responsibility to Power: Public Communication in Critical Times

Graham Murdock

When the publisher sent me the original proposal for *Power Without Responsibility* (*PWR*) to review, it was immediately clear it was a book whose time had come. It offered readers encountering media and communication studies for the first time a compelling narrative, detailing successive struggles around the organisation of the press and broadcasting and their central role in politics and collective life. The material was drawn mainly from British experience but the argument went to the heart of general debates and doubts about the constitution of capitalist democracies. Secondly, it spoke to a decisive shift in the political environment signalled by the election of Margaret Thatcher's first Conservative government in 1979 and the concerted assault on established conceptions of public service and the public interest mounted by champions of market fundamentalism and privatisation. Britain's experience was distinctive, shaped by a particular combination of historical forces, but marketisation, in various forms, was to gain global reach.

When *PWR* first appeared in 1981, media and communication studies was still mostly confined to the periphery of British academia outside the golden triangle of Oxford, Cambridge and London. The three foundational research centres were housed in provincial redbrick universities: the Centre for Television Research at Leeds, the Centre for Mass Communication Research at Leicester, and the Centre for Contemporary Cultural Studies at Birmingham. They were joined by the *Bad News* team at Glasgow University but research elsewhere was mostly taking place in what were then the 'new' universities built from scratch on greenfield sites. Notable contributions had come from Jeremy Tunstall and Stanley Cohen at Essex, Colin Seymore-Ure at Kent, and Simon Frith at Warwick. Undergraduate teaching, however, developed first in the polytechnics, traditionally the second English tier of higher education, led by the department at the Polytechnic of Central London (later to become Westminster University) headed by Nick Garnham. Alongside launching the first named degree in media and communication studies in 1975 the Central London department rapidly became a centre for cutting-edge research which, as James Curran (an early member of the department) noted, 'took the materialist road and grubbed around in the political economy of the media, its institutions, regulation, technology and history' (Curran 2004, 16). *PWR* assembled the scattered literatures in these areas and wove them into a compelling narrative that immediately engaged readers coming to the arguments for the first time. Its lucid exposition, attention to telling detail and moral vision secured a readership well beyond the walls of the university.

Emerging debates in media studies had already reached a wider audience through the third level course, Mass communication and Society, offered by the Open University, Britain's national degree awarding institution for adults studying part-time. James Curran was a member of the course team and the course itself ran from 1977 to 1983. A collection, with versions of the study materials (Gurevitch et al. 1982) and a second volume containing the key supporting readings were on general sale in bookshops (Curran et al. 1977). As Curran and his co-editor, Michael Gurevitch, later noted, the collected readings 'quickly reached an audience far wider than the one for which it was originally intended'—a success they rightly attributed 'to the manner in which the book succeeded, more or less by accident, in identifying and defining the contours of the field at the time' (Curran and Gurevitch 1991, 7).

The course team broke with the usual summative overview provided by introductory textbooks and organised the presentation of issues around the 'division and opposition between liberal pluralist and Marxist views of the media' (Gurevitch et al. 1982, 1). Inspired by Marxism and other currents of radical critique, British work in communication had begun to develop a critical political economy of communication. This placed uses and abuses of private power at the centre of analysis, went beyond and beneath events to analyse transformations unfolding over loops of time, and insisted on the moral obligation to support struggles to defend and extend a public communication system that promoted equity, justice and mutuality (Murdock and Golding 1974, 1977). *PWR* is animated by all three of these injunctions.

James Curran trained as a historian and took an early lead in promoting media history, at the time a relatively marginal specialism within historical scholarship. His jointly edited volume, *Newspaper History: From the Seventeenth Century to the Present Day* (Boyce, Curran and Wingate 1978) was a landmark contribution. The historical sweep of *PWR's* analysis of the commercial forces that have persistently blocked and marginalised the possibilities for a radical press is one of its enduring strengths.

This narrative is not simply a contribution to intellectual inquiry: it is also a call to arms. As Marx famously noted, exposing the roots of injustice, inequality and abuses of corporate power imposes a moral obligation to commit to struggles to rectify them. James Curran has heeded this injunction throughout his career.

He has been unswervingly committed to bringing academics, activists and trade unionists together to critique prevailing structures and advocate alternatives, a project exemplified in the essays collected in *The British Press: A Manifesto* (Curran 1978) and *Bending Reality: The State of the Media* (Curran et al. 1986), and in his founding editorship of the left Labour magazine, the *New Socialist,* launched in 1981. This had the declared intention of providing 'a bridge between public intellectuals, the Labour movement and radical civil society' (quoted in Frost 2020). *PWR* shares this ambition of reaching beyond the academy and contributing evidence and argument to the flow of political debate.

Both authors of *PWR* are notable public intellectuals. Since 2006 Jean Seaton has directed the Orwell Prize, Britain's premier annual award for political writing. Her current role as the BBC's official historian places her in the eye of the political storms raging around the Corporation's purpose and future, prompting deeply polarised reviews of her first volume, covering the period from 1970 to 1987 when marketisation was gathering momentum (Seaton 2016).

The tradition of political economy, which provides *PWR's* overarching conceptual framework, was grounded in moral philosophy from the outset. Adam Smith published his manifesto for a market-based capitalism, *The Wealth of Nations*, in 1776 within months of England's American colonies declaring independence from hereditary rule and founding a republic. This accident of historical timing ushered in a profound and enduring tension between two opposed conceptions of the good society. Smith placed freedom of personal choice at the centre of his vision of capitalism as a new moral social order. Entrepreneurs should be free to enter any market and compete for custom with the minimum of state interference and consumers should be free to choose between the maximum possible range of products designed to satisfy their needs and express their tastes and personalities. An automatic self-correcting mechanism, the market's celebrated 'hidden hand', would eliminate abuses of producer power.

Radical critics have persistently exposed this vision of minimally regulated 'free' market capitalism to relentless interrogation. They have repeatedly demonstrated that far from fostering open competition, it produces cumulative corporate concentration and entrenched regimes of private control. Rather than guaranteeing universal access to essential resources, it redirects wealth, income and opportunity to the top of the social scale cementing enduring inequalities and exclusions. Against these subversions of the common good, critical political economists follow the French Revolutionaries in demanding equality and mutuality as well as personal liberty and recasting democratic society as a collective of citizens, not an assembly of atomised consumers. Citizenship confers membership of a moral and political community based on a social contract that balances rights against responsibilities. Entitlements to the material and cultural resources required to live a full life carry with them a responsibility to contribute to the maintenance and vitality of the communal realm.

Communication systems play pivotal roles in supporting this social contract. They provide infrastructures of connection that sustain personal and collective contact over time and space. They manufacture and distribute information, analysis, fictions, and imagery offering competing understandings and misunderstandings of the prevailing social order and stage dramatisations and debates on the options for personal agency and social change.

As the historical account in *PWR* demonstrates with exemplary clarity, communication markets, left to their own devices, have signally failed to serve the interests of citizenship. Private ownership, profit maximisation and commercial logic have proved unable and unwilling to provide the range of cultural and informational resources required to support full social and political participation on a basis of equity. Corporate interests and logics persistently marginalise and denigrate alternatives to 'business as usual' proposed by organised labour and social movements.

By insistently celebrating the identity of consumer and promoting personal market choices as the preeminent arena of personal expression and self-realisation, commercial provision systematically devalues and marginalises citizenship's commitment to contribute to the quality of public life.

These manifest market failures have prompted two major responses from democratic governments: strong public interest regulation of market structures and corporate action, and public ownership and management of key communication facilities. Britain's postwar telecommunications network was a nationalised industry with subsidised domestic call charges and public telephone boxes to ensure maximum social access. Until the introduction of commercial television in the mid-1950s, broadcasting was a public service monopoly vested in the British Broadcasting Corporation (BBC) paid for out of the public purse and barred from accepting commercial advertising. Over 18 years, from 1979 to 1997, Conservative governments led by Margaret Thatcher and her successors pursued a comprehensive program of marketisation, opening previously restricted markets to competition (liberalisation), selling public assets to private investors (privatisation), weakening or removing public interest regulations restricting corporate action (re-regulation), and pressuring public institutions to behave more like profit-seeking enterprises (corporatisation).

In 1981, the telecommunications network was opened to competition followed in 1984 by the initial sale of BT shares to private investors. The BBC avoided privatisation but faced significant new competition for audiences. In 1984, the cable television industry, previously confined to relaying the main terrestrial broadcast services, was freed to offer additional channels. In 1990, following the collapse of the consortium awarded the original franchise, which had included the BBC, Rupert Murdoch assumed monopoly control over British satellite television services. The BBC was placed under further pressure by successive real cuts to its licence fee funding and demands to maximise additional revenues by pursuing a more entrepreneurial strategy. After an acrimonious debate, however, public service provision was unexpectedly extended in November 1982 with the launch of Channel 4. The new channel was funded by advertising but with a remit to serve minority interests and foster innovation by commissioning almost all of its programming from a diverse group of independent producers.

In contrast, the national press saw significant further consolidation when, in 1981, Rupert Murdoch's bid to acquire the *Times* and *Sunday*

Times was officially approved giving him a significant stake in the broadsheet market to add to the domination of the tabloid market he already enjoyed through his ownership of the *Sun* and *The News of the World* and an almost 40% share of the national newspaper market overall.

Against this relentless push to corporate capture and enclosure, *PWR* spoke responsibility to power issuing a clarion call for democratic governments to honour the promise of citizenship by ensuring that the cultural and informational resources and spaces required for full social participation are equally open to all and are not commandeered or subverted by the priorities and practices of private capital and commercialism.

The early editions responded to marketisation's mission to reconstruct the communications landscape by calling for a new integrated government ministry 'responsible not only for the mass media but also for the post, telephone and the emerging technologies of information… that could properly consider the political and economic implications of… the increased concentration of economic power across all the media by a few large companies' (Curran and Seaton 1985, 330–331). Strong public interest regulation of private corporations is absolutely necessary and, faced with the unprecedented power of the dominant digital platforms, more pressing than ever, but it is not enough. There needs to be an organised countervailing force to commercialism, funded out of taxation, not reliant on advertising revenues or customer subscriptions, operating at arm's length from government and committed to public provision in support of citizenship. The task of constructing this space in Britain has fallen to the BBC but, as Seaton's chapters on the Corporation's institutional career in *PWR* demonstrate, it was a project cross cut with tensions from the outset. By the time the book's second edition appeared in 1985, it was apparent that in a rapidly changing operating environment broadcasting needed 'to find a …new form of commitment to public service' (Curran and Seaton 1985, 314).

From the mid-1990s onwards, broadcasting's privileged position as the primary public medium faced a concerted challenge from the World Wide Web. With the launch of Apple's iPhone in the summer of 2007 and the rapid roll-out of always on/always there smartphones, digital access became a ubiquitous focus of everyday communicative activity. By then the internet's core uses had been comprehensively captured and enclosed by a handful of commercial companies, based offshore in the United States, and claiming monopoly rights to harvest, analyse and sell users' personal data to direct sales and advertising more effectively. Amazon, launched in 1994, dominated online shopping; Google, launched in 1998, dominated search; and Facebook, launched in 2006, rapidly became the dominant social media platform. Under their combined influence, the public internet was reorganised as a massive new engine of targeted advertising driving increasing levels of environmentally destructive hyper-consumption.

The original utopian vision of the internet as an open public space of exploration and participation rapidly receded but did not entirely disappear. Public cultural institutions, museums, libraries, archives, galleries, university research repositories and public broadcasters, digitised their holdings and expertise and experimented with new ways of interacting with audiences. A wealth of publicly paid for resources, previously only accessible at specified locations and times, became openly available online. At the same time, voluntary collaborative initiatives were producing new free-to-use cultural resources, Wikipedia being the best known. Taken together, digital public cultural goods, paid for out of taxation, and gift economies supported by donated money, time and expertise, offered not-for-profit counterweights to the commercial platform corporations. Debate on the meaning and organisation of public service shifted from its historic focus on public service broadcasting (PSB) to arguments around the possibility of building a more general public service media (PSM) system, raising central questions around the future relationship between public service broadcasting and a public service internet (see Fuchs and Unterberger 2021).

The later editions of *PWR* include 'new media' as a third major focus, alongside the press and broadcasting. Drawing on the analysis developed by James and his Goldsmiths colleagues in *Misunderstanding the Internet* (Curran, Fenton and Freedman 2016), the additional chapters offer one of the clearest accounts we have of the World Wide Web's corruption by commerce. As Curran notes in a recent contribution: 'It is time that we consider how the gains of digitalisation can be harvested for the public good' (Curran 2022, 53).

His preferred option is the creation of a British Digital Corporation, an idea initially floated by the former editor of *The Times*, James Harding, and endorsed by the former leader of the Labour Party, Jeremy Corbyn. Funded by a levy on the advertising revenues of digital companies with a more than 25% share of online search and social networking markets, the new Corporation would 'create and fund an independent media sector producing output with a public purpose… from films, TV programmes, websites and print publications to video games' (Curran 2022, 54). It would operate alongside but separate from the BBC which Curran argues is too 'anchored in the political class', increasingly wedded to a 'market-oriented corporate culture' and needs to be 'shaken up by competition from an innovative and autonomous rival better reflecting the diversity of British society' (ibid.). A similar vision underpins recent proposals for the creation of 'a well-resourced independent Media Commons—a thriving ecology of participatory newsrooms, community radio stations, digital innovators and cultural producers which can sit alongside transformed legacy public service media institutions, collaborate with them and hold them to account (Media Reform Coalition 2021).

Neither of these proposals has much to say about the essential contribution of public cultural institutions outside the media system. Any plan for digitalising public service requires a strategy for making the wealth of cultural and information resources offered by public libraries, museums, universities, archives, galleries and performance spaces more readily visible and accessible. Which bring us to the problem of distribution and search. In making the case for a British Digital Corporation, Curran insists that it would be required to 'commission a set proportion of their qualifying content from programmes funded by the BDC to *prevent its marginalisation*' (Curran 2022, 53—italics added). This rider concedes the BBC's continuing centrality in national cultural life. There is, therefore, a strong argument for capitalising on this and repositioning the BBC as the pivotal node in a public service digital network mediating access to the online resources offered by both public cultural institutions and collaborative gift economies through a public search engine that prioritises social value (see Murdock 2021).

Under current conditions, however, arguments over how best to embed a revitalised conception of public service for digital times at the centre of popular communication must, as a matter of urgency, also confront the escalating climate and environmental emergencies. Digital communication systems, however organised, depend on a thickening infrastructural network of transmitters, cables and satellites, and a proliferating array of production equipment and consumer devices. These very material formations currently depend on modes of mineral extraction, manufacture, transportation, energy use and disposal that cause cumulative environmental damage and all too often depend on labour exploitation. No matter how democratically organised, socially inclusive, committed to providing a platform for marginalised voices, and innovative in the forms of representation it employs, any proposal for alternative communications that fails to confront these realities colludes by default with the spoliations and dispossessions of an economic system constructed around corporate interests and ambitions.

Acknowledging this imposes three immediate priorities. First, eliminating climate destructive emissions from every stage of cultural production and use by moving to clean energy, retrofitting buildings, rethinking transportation needs and promoting repair and reuse. Second, ensuring that none of the equipment used in public communication relies on labour exploitation at any point in its chains of production. And third, developing future infrastructures, operating systems and devices that are environmentally and socially positive.

Given the concerted corporate push to promote the next generation of digital technologies, organised around artificial intelligence and the immersive internet, the Metaverse, any movement to achieve these goals must enlist in struggles to wrest effective control of technological innovation away from the major digital platforms and take an active role in developing communication infrastructures and devices that meet public needs without fuelling climate and environmental crises and social exploitation.

To speak responsibility to power at this present juncture in history is necessarily also to speak of care for the natural world and for the lives and life chances of distant others.

References

Boyce, G., Curran, J., and Wingate P. (Eds.) 1978. *Newspaper History: From the 17th Century to the Present Day.* Constable.

Curran, J. (Ed.) 1978. *The British Press: A Manifesto.* Macmillan Press.

Curran, J. 2004. The Rise of the Westminster School. In A. Calabrese and C. Sparks (Eds.) *Towards a Political Economy of Culture: Capitalism and Communication in the Twenty-First Century,* pp. 13–40. Rowman and Littlefield.

Curran, J. 2022. An End to Futility: A Modest Proposal. In J. Zylinska (Ed.) *The Future of Media,* pp. 45–56. Goldsmiths Press.

Curran, J., Ecclestone, J., Oakley, G. and Richardson, A. (Eds.) 1986. *Bending Reality: The State of the Media.* Pluto Press.

Curran, J., Gurevitch, M. and Wollacott, J. (Eds.) 1977. *Mass Communication and Society.* Edward Arnold in Association with the Open University.

Curran, J. and Gurevitch, M. (Eds.) 1991. Introduction. In J. Curran and M. Gurevitch (Eds.) *Mass Media and Society*, pp. 7–11. Edward Arnold.

Curran, J. and Seaton, J. 1985. *Power Without Responsibility: The Press and Broadcasting in Britain*, 2nd edition. Methuen.

Frost, D. 2020. The First New Socialist. 25 August. http://newsocialist,org.uk/first-new-socialist. Accessed June 18 2022

Fuchs, C. and Unterberger, K. (Eds.) 2021. *The Public Service Media and the Public Service Internet Manifesto*. University of Westminster Press.

Gurevich, M., Bennett, T., Curran, J. and Woollacott, J. 1982. Preface. In M. Gurevitch, T. Bennett, J. Curran and J. Woollacott (Eds.). *Culture, Media and Society*, pp. 1–3. Methuen.

Media Reform Coalition. 2021. *Manifesto for a People's Media: Creating a Media Commons*. Media Reform Coalition. https://www.mediareform.org.uk/get-involved/manifesto-for-a-peoples-media

Murdock, G. 2021. Public Service Media for Critical Times: Connectivity, Climate and Corona. In C. Fuchs and K. Unterberger (Eds.) *The Public Service Media and Public Service Internet Manifesto*, pp. 69–111. University of Westminster Press.

Murdock, G. and Golding, P. 1974. For a Political Economy of Mass Communications. In R. Miliband and J. Saville (Eds.) *The Socialist Register 1973*, pp. 205–234. The Merlin Press.

Murdock, G. and Golding, P. 1977. Capitalism, Communication and Class Relations. In J. Curran, M. Gurevitch and J. Woollacott (Eds.) *Mass Communication and Society*, pp. 12–43. Edward Arnold.

Seaton, J. 2015. *Pinkoes and Traitors: The BBC and the Nation 1970–1987*. Profile Books.

CHAPTER 20

'SMET' and the BBC

Patrick Barwise

My perspective on media is both consistent with, and complementary to, that of *Power Without Responsibility*.

Consistent because my work, too, is empirical, cross-disciplinary and, broadly, social-democratic. Jean Seaton and I are invariably on the same side of the barricades in debates about the BBC and *PWR*'s description of it as 'an imperfect beauty' is exactly the way I see it. (To which I'd add that it's also extremely difficult to help: being a genuine critical friend of the BBC has been a pretty tough gig.)

Complementary because my main focus has always been on *audiences, economics* and, to a lesser extent, *technologies*, although working on *The War Against the BBC* (Barwise and York 2020), I also got into media *content, power and politics*—central concerns in *PWR*—more than in my previous work.

My media research and policy work mainly relate to the issues in part two of *PWR*—broadcasting—including the role of the right-wing press in the 'war' against the BBC. When Peter York and I started our research for our book, we had two rather tacit assumptions about all this.

First, we thought that, among the wider public, those who leant to the right would see the BBC as left-leaning, especially if they were older and socially conservative, and that younger, socially liberal, left-leaning people would see it as pro-establishment and somewhat right-leaning. That assumption turned out to be largely correct.

Second, we thought that the organised, professional attacks on the BBC (i.e. by people *as part of their day jobs*) would be *a bit* more from the right. We were wrong about that: organised Beeb-bashing by think tanks, politicians and journalists is *overwhelmingly* from the right. Which brings us closer to the issues in *PWR*.

We think there are several reasons for this imbalance.

- *Commercial vested interests*—notably the BBC's biggest enemy, Rupert Murdoch—are mostly right-leaning.
- *Free-market ideology*: hence the attacks by think tanks like the Institute for Economic Affairs and the Adam Smith Institute, now amplified by culture warriors like the New Culture Forum (although, in reality, Netflix is *much* more 'woke' than the Beeb) (Barwise and York 2020, 128–129)
- Our impression is that those who lean to the right are more likely to think most other people agree with them—the *'silent majority' illusion* (ibid., 124–125)
- *Resources*: the right-wing think tanks are much better—and more opaquely—funded than those on the left (ibid., 105–117)
- And *the press*, especially 'SMET'—the *Sun, Mail, Express* and *Telegraph*—is mostly right-leaning (ibid., 143–5 and chapter 7). (Interestingly, not so much the *Times* and *Sunday Times*, which—despite being part of the Murdoch empire—have a much more independent and balanced editorial position than the SMET papers, presumably for reputational reasons.)

On the BBC's supposed left-wing bias, we drew on two important sources:

- *Academic research*, especially by the Cardiff University group (ibid., Chapter 9 and Appendix B).
- And *the British public*, who must be a great disappointment to those peddling the 'left-wing BBC' narrative.

It is true that much of the public—about 20%—agrees with that narrative. But an equal number think the opposite and the 60% in between either explicitly say the BBC is balanced or respond 'Don't know', which is hardly consistent with the 'left-wing BBC' narrative. And, when asked which *one* source they turn to for trusted news, 51% said the BBC, versus only about 1% for each of the SMET papers. The second most-cited source was ITN on 9% (ibid., 237–241).

In that sense, the 'war on the BBC' has failed to persuade the public not to trust it.

What is less clear is whether the constant right-wing attacks have made the BBC unduly cautious in covering stories the government would prefer to bury (ibid., 158–161). We think yes but, anecdotally, this is contested by people at the BBC and it certainly doesn't seem to be about explicit, top-down censorship.

More clear-cut is the evidence that the two big *economic* criticisms of the BBC are nonsense.

One of these, much favoured by Rupert and James Murdoch, is that the BBC actually *reduces consumer choice by crowding out commercial provision*. There has never been any evidence to support this claim and there is now a lot of evidence against it (ibid., chapter 11 and appendix E).

The other economic criticism is that the BBC provides *poor value for money*. In 2015, the Corporation ran an experiment focusing on the large minority of licence payers who think this, getting them to live with no BBC services for nine days. At the end of the nine days, two-thirds had changed their minds (ibid., 32–4 and appendix A). In April 2022, the BBC released the results of a replication of this study, which produced *identical* results (BBC, 2022). But do not expect to see this widely reported in the SMET papers.

References

Barwise, P., and York, P. 2020. *The War Against the BBC*. Penguin.
BBC 2022. BBC publishes results of deprivation study. BBC press office. https://www.bbc.co.uk/mediacentre/2022/deprivation-study accessed 5 January 2024.

CHAPTER 21

The Power and Responsibility to Emancipate Audiences: A Reflection on Public Service Media's Role in Democratic Societies

Karen Donders[1]

Public service media organisations have always been at the centre of Western European media systems. The early days of radio technology are the exception to that rule. But, essentially broadcasting has been dominated by public institutions such as the BBC, ARD or Flemish VRT for decades. The importance of public service media was of a societal, creative and economic nature. Indeed, because of their reach, high market shares and public funding, public service media organisations have not only been able to deliver highly valuable public services to audiences but have additionally put their mark on the economic development of media markets. Even the arrival of profit-driven competitors did not change that. Yes, they ended monopoly, which was a good thing for citizens, but also for public service media organisations who had to reinvent themselves and to become more consumer-centric and less driven by politics and bureaucracy.

Today, public broadcasters are still vital for democracy. Despite their flaws, they meaningfully contribute to informed, social and cultural citizenship. The essential conditions for this to occur are accountability, transparency, professionalism, adaptivity and the ethical behavior of public broadcasters. Most importantly, public broadcasters have to think less about their own problems and instead need to act on the basis of what is best for their societies. Governments, meanwhile, need to ensure adequate funding, effective oversight and evaluation, and meaningful independence from political and market pressures. Both sides need to put their trust in public service media as key not only to media systems, but to democracies in general (Donders 2021).

We are all aware that the conditions briefly pointed out above should not be taken for granted. While public broadcasters struggle to remain relevant as they face a significant decline in audiences, limits to the expansion of their digital activities, and both internal and external pressures to evolve into more adaptable public organisations, governments consistently decrease funding and seem more concerned with the development of a highly consolidated and profitable media market. In my experience, public broadcasters are, on the one hand, seen as too conservative and elitist while on the other, are simultaneously described by their critics as socialist, progressive and even 'woke' (see also Donders 2021, 64–67).

It is within this context that the work of James Curran and Jean Seaton's *Power Without Responsibility* (2018) remains seminal. While a lot of us, and rightly so, focus on the agency of users and specifically the opportunities that digitisation offers in this regard, Curran and Seaton present us with one of the most comprehensive analyses of the UK media system. They do so from a combined historical, sociological, political and structural/economic angle and, in later editions of their work, they compellingly illustrate the persistence of mechanisms of power, repression and manipulation. I will reflect on that observation below. Does power come with or without responsibility? And what does that mean for public service media organisations?

Public service broadcasting started as a project of political power maximisation. Scholars including Eli Noam (1995) and Wolfgang Hoffmann-Riem (1991) have illustrated this to be the case in most Western European countries. Having said that, the policy project was, from the outset, also one with citizen emancipation at its core. Graham Murdock (2005, 178) contends that media ought to be 'a ladder which people could steadily climb, moving from the lowest rungs of packaged commercial entertainment to the highest rungs of consecrated cultural artefacts'. Public broadcasters, being independent from politics and markets, had to make that happen. They had to address people as citizens instead of consumers and, as in the words of Jay Blumler (1992, 14), to take 'responsibility for the health of the political process and for the quality of public discourse generated with it'. The question for today is whether public broadcasters still have the power to achieve such enormous aspirations and, if so, whether they remain equipped and committed to take up that responsibility.

In my book *Public Service Media in Europe: Law, Theory and Practice* (Donders 2021), I argue that public broadcasters do indeed have powers to transform societies and markets. Inspired by the work of Hilde Van den Bulck (2016) and Peter Dahlgren (1995), I make a distinction between public broadcasters' contribution to political, social, cultural and civic citizenship. In all of these domains, Western European public broadcasters can make and have made valuable contributions. Admittedly, at times they have also failed, adding to polarisation of political debate, inadequately representing the diversity of opinions in society, or informing only certain parts of the audience—notably those that are better educated.

Some would argue that public broadcasters, at least in terms of output, still achieve their objectives but miss out on impact because of their decreasing reach. That is indeed a major problem. Although public broadcasters should not strive after high market shares at all cost, reach is a quintessential condition for output to result in impact. Let me make two rather different assessments. First, public broadcasters still reach almost the entire population on a weekly basis. There is not a single social media platform that can say the same (although internet giants such as Google do have this level of reach in many countries). Hence, public broadcasters are still very powerful actors in media systems. Second, and in contrast, public broadcasters' reach with younger people and people with ethnically diverse backgrounds is consistently lower across Western Europe than overall reach and shows a consistent trend of decline. Consumption volume in age groups younger than 35 drops dramatically. For example, the public broadcaster I am working for, VRT, saw daily viewing time in the 25–34 age group drop from 35.5 minutes in 2013 to 22.3 minutes in 2022, a loss of 37% over a ten-year period. In the 13–24 year group, the decline is even more dramatic, with daily viewing time halving during this period (down 49%).[2] According to internal VRT research, these groups consume a significant amount of content on our digital platform, VRT MAX, but still far from the amount of time that they used to spend on our linear television channels. For radio, the situation is even worse. Our youth-oriented radio channel lost 25% of its market share in 2021 although website, app and social media consumption provides at least some compensation. When you take such figures into account, it is clear that while public broadcasters still have the power to be relevant, they need to become genuine public service media organisations or even public service platforms if they are to remain relevant and sustainable.

The turn from a public broadcaster to a public service media organisation or platform has been evident since the millennium, but is difficult to achieve. Public broadcasters themselves are quite static organisations; staff do not always have the right competencies, and governments have definitely not taken up their responsibliity to facilitate the shift to a more sustainable public service model in media. They continue to consistently cut funding and adopt regulation that favours private sector expansion over public service media adaptation. Most current regulation still regards digital services as an add-on—an accessory activity for public service media organisations—instead of recognising them as core to their future sustainability.

The answer to the question as to whether public broadcasters still have the power to be relevant is thus mixed. Public broadcasters still reach a lot of people, contribute to informed citizenship, place otherwise marginalised topics on the political agenda, enhance empathy between communities, raise attention for the arts, and invest in innovation (see several contributions in Puppis and Ali 2021). At the same time, one can hardly be blind to the fact that most public broadcasters lag behind in the digital platform world because of their own inefficiencies and insecurities and because of political elites' resistance to accelerating the transition from public service broadcasting to public service media.

Indeed, it is hard to deny that the digital platform environment in which we live is based on the further commodification of audiences, a lack of transparency in the use of our data, and an intensified consolidation of media ownership structures exemplified by the domination of a handful of tech giants over the digital landscape. In this situation, let us assume that, for the next decade or so, public broadcasters still have the power to impact societies in a context in which the public interest matters more than ever.

To what extent do public broadcasters actively seek to enhance citizenship? My argument would be that most public broadcasters in Western Europe at least try to do that: admittedly, they do an imperfect job, but they often give it their best shot.

I would like to illustrate this by giving two examples related to the Flemish public broadcaster VRT where I now work. These examples are not an exhaustive overview of who we are and what we do. Rather, they show how we reflect on our role and power in society and try to be responsible. The first example relates to our policies to reach all people in society, regardless of age, gender, education background and so forth. To make this happen we work together with organisations that specialise in accessible language use. We ensure our news broadcasts on television and radio and our news website can be understood by as many people as possible. We have a panel of 1,000 people that we interrogate every single day for their reflections on our news offer. That does not only relate to language, but also to our choice of topics and the way we cover the news. Journalists still make editorial choices on their own: that is their responsibility. But they actively listen—more so than before—to their audiences.

We also make sure that we represent different people on screen. We are not there yet, but we at least aim to reflect all people in society, across age, gender, ethnicity, economic conditions and disability. When we make musicals for children, we look for talent everywhere and make sure that children who do not have the means to go to the set are driven there. We provide intense year-long internships to people from urban communities and provide opportunities to digital talent who may not have the 'right' degree but who have clear potential to develop in our company or elsewhere in the media sector. We invite people with disabilities to explain to our content makers how they view our programmes and we adjust our content, not because we have to but because we choose to be inspired to do so.

The second example concerns our approach as to how we use social media to extend the reach and impact of our news output. For example, we actively make use of Instagram and TikTok because children and young people care about the news, but they have different (and higher) expectations than older audiences. In general, they do not like political brawls, endless pessimism and insulting exchanges. They still insist on trustworthy news, independence and quality. That is why we invest in social media content that focuses on news that is relevant to their lives; we interact and find out what is going on in the lives of teenagers. If they believe that the Covid vaccine will make their breasts bigger, we ask our science journalists to find out whether that is true and our young, digital journalists make an easy-to-understand item exploring this issue. If somebody misbehaves in the chat, we delete their response and let them know personally why we did that. It works. We reach a lot of youngsters this way. Actually, our Instagram brand NWS.NWS.NWS is the most well-known VRT brand among young people.

I have dozens more examples to share, all of which reveal that, when we are committed to our ideals and do not forget the DNA of who we are, we can both have the power to impact society and be responsible when we act.

We are not passive victims of politicians when exerting that power. Public broadcasters are living organisms with people making choices on a daily basis that make us less or more public service media.

Notes

1 This chapter represents the opinions of the author and not those of VRT.
2 The figures are based on an analysis by the VRT research department of the official Belgian CIM TV data (https://www.cim.be).

References

Blumler, J. 1992. *Television and the Public Interest*. Sage.
Curran, J. and Seaton, J. 2018. *Power Without Responsibility: Press, Broadcasting and the Internet in Britain*, 8th edition. Routledge.
Dahlgren, P. 1995. *Television and the Public Sphere*. Sage.
Donders, K. 2021. *Public Service Media in Europe: Law, Theory and Practice*. Routledge.
Hoffmann-Riem, W. 1991. Rundfunk als public service—ein überholtes Konzept?. In R. Weiss (Ed.), *Aufgaben und Perspektiven des öffentlich-rechtlichen Fernsehens* (pp. 21–47). Nomos.
Murdock, G. 2005. Building the Digital Commons: Public Broadcasting in the Age of the Internet. In G.F. Lowe and P. Jauert (Eds.), *Cultural Dilemmas in Public Service Broadcasting* (pp. 213–230). Nordicom.
Noam, E. 1995. *Television in Europe*. Oxford University Press.
Puppis, M. and Ali, C. (Eds.) 2021. *Public Service Media's Contribution to Society*. Nordicom.
Van den Bulck, H. 2016. *Publieke omroep: Maatschappelijke meerwaarde en indi-viduele impact*. University of Antwerp.

CHAPTER 22

Public Service, Technology and Innovation

Michael Klontzas

It is not surprising that much of media scholarship concentrates on the political, social and cultural significance of the media. Histories of the press, broadcasting and 'new media' also account for the impact of technological change on production, distribution and consumption. *Power Without Responsibility* pioneered this tradition, creating the blueprint for others to follow.

There is, however, another aspect that is often downplayed: how public funding and particular institutional configurations stimulate technological innovation that shapes our public communications infrastructure. *PWR* does not explicitly frame this as a distinct theme, but it should be credited with providing evidence of how certain key technologies have been the product of public intervention. Taking a more critical approach, Seaton dismisses the technological determinism of 'neophiliacs and cultural pessimists' (Curran and Seaton 1997, 208), recognises that broadcasting was a social rather than a technical invention (1997, 112), and in so doing unpacks how radical shifts in the media were not merely the product of inescapable, linear progress, lone inventors, entrepreneurship or market forces.

In his history of the internet, added to *PWR* more recently as the revised chapter that first appeared in *Misunderstanding the Internet* (Curran et al. 2012), Curran explains how the birth of the ubiquitous digital network that we now take for granted can be traced back to the US Department of Defense responding to the imminent threat of a nuclear attack by the USSR in the Cold War era. Sustained government funding saw the creation of ARPANET, a resilient communications infrastructure driven by military priorities. However, referring to the culture of the scientific community who designed the technology, Curran insightfully goes on to say that '[t]he internet was the product not only of human ingenuity and state money, but also of the values of the people who first developed it' (Curran and Seaton 2018, 364). He then identifies the formative influence of the American counterculture in the 1980s, followed by the effects of the European public service tradition and commercialisation.

This interplay between structure and agency in the context of institutions, defined by Selznick (1957) as organisations 'infused with value', provides a powerful lens that reveals how 'cognitive scripts' constrain and condition perceptions of what constitutes legitimate means and ends (Hall and Taylor 1996), and how a public interest ethos in public mission driven institutions shape emerging media and communications technologies. Seaton applies a similar approach to the BBC when she defines the broadcaster as 'a set of values embodied in considered and evolving practices which it can use to re-engineer public life in the interests of the public' (Curran and Seaton 2018, 338). She argues that since the 1990s, 'the Corporation has been a leading market maker in technological innovation'. It adopted a distribution technology agnosticism in reaching its audience over all new digital satellite, cable and digital terrestrial transmission platforms, and in doing so supported their growth. It offered iPlayer, its pioneering video-on-demand service that established television programme streaming and created a market for commercial players (2018, 340). In the wake of the ITV Digital demise in 2002, it led the key initiative to launch Freeview, a popular free digital offering and an alternative to satellite and cable pay television. That move rescued the Digital Terrestrial Television (DTT) platform which was an essential public policy requirement before the government could initiate switching off analogue television broadcasting and reap the benefits of digital convergence in advanced communications services (2018, 352–3).

These are striking examples of how the BBC has been leading technical innovation, but they are part of a much broader picture. The BBC's engagement with DTT can be traced back to the early 1990s technical feasibility studies, run by the then regulator for commercial television, Independent Television Commission (ITC), and the BBC itself. Subsequently, it contributed to the European Digital Video Broadcasting project that created the DVB-T transmission standard for DTT (British Broadcasting Corporation 1992; Starks 2007, 27–31). By launching its Digital Audio Broadcast (DAB) service in 1995, when there was hardly an audience, the BBC singlehandedly drove digital radio out of the vicious circle produced by the reluctance of audiences, commercial broadcasters and electronic equipment manufacturers to make the first move. BBC Online, formerly BBCi, was praised for boosting the take-up of the internet in the UK (Klontzas 2013). Four years before Netflix launched its streaming service in the UK, the Corporation spearheaded the proposed Project Kangaroo, a joint video-on-demand platform bringing together the back catalogues of the major public service broadcasters in the UK—the BBC, ITV and Channel 4. The following year, in 2009, this was blocked by the Competition Commission, and later resurfaced as Project Canvas, YouView and Britbox.

The list of BBC's digital initiatives is very long, and its commitment to mobilising its tangible and intangible resources to support building digital Britain made its way into its renewed remit in 2006 as its sixth public purpose:

> ...helping to deliver to the public the benefit of emerging communications technologies and services and, in addition, taking a leading role in the switchover to digital television. (Department for Culture, Media and Sport 2006)

But the BBC has always been an inventor and an innovator. With a proud tradition of in-house engineering, and an internationally renowned Research & Development department, it carried out pioneering research into technologies that often satisfied narrow operational demands, such as designing new equipment, or created new ways to reach its licence fee payers (Shacklady and Ellen 2003). The ways in which this innovation historically spills over into the broader industry and produces amplified societal and economic impact, or 'public value', to use a more recent term, should not be underestimated. For instance, the first teletext service in the world, BBC's Ceefax, a text-based information service utilising spare transmission capacity on BBC channels, was almost immediately replicated by the ITV companies, BBC's commercial rivals, in advertising-funded Oracle, and public service broadcasters across Europe. It improved the utility of television for viewers, created a market for teletext services, and secured a virtual monopoly for the British standard around the world (Moe and Van den Bulck 2016; Schlesinger 1985).

The broader implications of the BBC's initiatives can be vividly seen in its Computer Literacy Project (CLP) in the early 1980s. The story of the BBC Microcomputer, emblematic of the project and so fondly remembered by many British who were schoolchildren then and are now in their fifties, has been told repeatedly. It was even immortalised in BBC 4's docudrama *Micro Men* in 2009 (BBC 2009; Blyth 2012). The real significance of CLP, however, lies in that it reveals how the self-identity of the Corporation and the individuals working for it was consistent with a set of values and a sense of mission to serve the public.

The BBC was among the first to draw attention to the implications of microelectronics for national competitiveness, employment and society at large. Amidst growing public concern, it launched its CLP as an awareness-raising campaign that dovetailed with an array of government initiatives promoting the rapid development, deployment and adoption of microcomputing technologies in schools, businesses, manufacturing and the home. In line with its legitimising remit, BBC departments came together to follow the lead of Continuing Education, Television (CET) in its ambitious plan to produce a television series supported with publications, software, advisory services and the endorsed BBC Microcomputer.

The capacity of the broadcaster to sense the changing environment, mobilise its significant tangible and intangible resources, liaise with external expertise and stakeholders, and mount a response to the perceived social needs for computer literacy in the public interest underpin the institutional embeddedness of the BBC and highlight its role as the cornerstone of a 'national system of innovation' (Mazzucato 2013, 2014) with demonstrable immediate and longer-term social and market impacts. While it becomes clear on closer inspection that the BBC did not behave as a monolithic organisation, and that radical initiatives can be traced back to individuals, the normative and structural features of the institution provide a unifying, legitimising narrative and the necessary enabling framework for agency.

PWR shines a light on how public institutions play a key role in developing communication infrastructures with lasting ripple effects that deliver multiplied social and economic benefits. What fuels this innovativeness is a shared public service ethos within institutions such as public service media and public universities, and common understandings of what is appropriate beyond market logics. Undermining such institutions or subordinating them to wholesale marketisation amounts to losing our ability for long-term, socially beneficial blue skies innovation when uncertainty and investment risk are high.

References

BBC 2009. *Micro Men*, programme transmitted 8 October, https://www.bbc.co.uk/programmes/b00n5b92

Blyth, T. 2012. *The Legacy of the BBC Micro: Effecting Change in the UK's Cultures of Computing*. Nesta and Science Museum.

British Broadcasting Corporation. 1992. *Extending Choice: The BBC's Role in the New Broadcasting Age*. British Broadcasting Corporation.

Curran, J., Fenton, N. and Freedman, D. 2012. *Misunderstanding the Internet*. Routledge.

Curran, J. and Seaton, J. 2018. *Power Without Responsibility: Press, Broadcasting and the Internet in Britain*, 8th edition. Routledge.

Curran, J. and Seaton, J. 1997. *Power Without Responsibility: The Press and Broadcasting in Britain*, 5th edition. Routledge.

Department for Culture, Media and Sport 2006. *Broadcasting – Copy of Royal Charter for the Continuance of the British Broadcasting Corporation* (Cm 6925).

Hall, P.A. and Taylor, R.C. 1996. Political Science and the Three New Institutionalisms. *Political Studies*, 44, 936–957. https://doi.org/10.1111/j.1467-9248.1996.tb00343.x

Klontzas, M. 2013. The BBC and Digital Policy Instrumentation in the UK: Straitjackets and Conveyor Belts. *International Journal of Digital Television*, 4, 49–65. https://doi.org/10.1386/jdtv.4.1.49_1

Mazzucato, M. 2014. *The Entrepreneurial State: Debunking Public vs. Private Sector Myths*, revised edition. Anthem Press.

Mazzucato, M. 2013. BBC: From Crowding Out to Dynamising In. In R. G. Picard and P. Siciliani (Eds.), *Is There Still a Place for Public Service Television: Effects of the Changing Economics of Broadcasting* (pp. 51–56). Reuters Institute for the Study of Journalism.

Moe, H. and Van den Bulck, H. (Eds.) 2016. *Teletext in Europe: From the Analog to the Digital Era*. Nordicom.

Schlesinger, P. 1985. From Public Service to Commodity: The Political Economy of Teletext in the UK. *Media, Culture & Society*, 7, 471–485. https://doi.org/10.1177/016344385007004005

Selznick, P. 1957. *Leadership in Administration: A Sociological Interpretation*. Row, Peterson.

Shacklady, N. and Ellen, M. 2003. *On Air: A History of BBC Transmission*. Wavechange Books.

Starks, M. 2007. *Switching to Digital Television: UK Public Policy and the Market*. Intellect.

Part V

Radical Journalism: Then and Now

Radical Journalism and *PWR*: Some Lessons from the Founding of the *Manchester Guardian*

Des Freedman

Back in the 1980s I was an aspiring independent documentary filmmaker and, when that failed, a news researcher at ITN. The first two books on the media that I bought were Stuart Hood's *On Television* (Hood 1980) and *Power Without Responsibility* (*PWR*) (Curran and Seaton 2018). As an eager and active socialist, I found the account in *PWR* of the rise of the unstamped newspapers in the 1830s (along with Stanley Harrison's *Poor Men's Guardians* [Harrison 1974] which I read later) totally inspiring. It was one of the first historical pieces of evidence for me about the potential of radical ideas to reach large audiences on the back of mass movements. *PWR* is the opposite of a dry and indifferent history and contains in that first section a fantastic account of the organising and 'mobilizing' power, of the press—in this case both amplifying and cementing the ideas of the Chartist movement in the UK in the 1830s and 1840s. This was a proper radical press: one that was committed to fostering activism—to active production, distribution and consumption—and dedicated to challenging existing social conditions. 'The rise of the militant press' argues *PWR*, 'fostered the development of a radical subculture, posing a challenge to the undemocratic social order' (Curran and Seaton 2018, 17). This seemed like good sense to me but to have a richly argued historical account was like gold dust.

I loved the sense of agency within this account: the idea that it was the growth of trade union and working-class political organisations that facilitated the growth of the radical press. Journalists and editors saw themselves as political activists rather than professional journalists without a stake in the issues. The scale of the movement in the 1830s meant that there was sufficient revenue from sales alone so that they didn't have to rely on advertising and the potential compromises and demographic temptations that advertising brings. As *PWR* puts it, 'independence from advertising was a liberating force' (ibid., 13)—exactly the opposite of the mainstream liberal argument, which *PWR* acknowledges at the very start, that it was advertising itself that freed the press from state control.

PWR argues that the militant press didn't collapse simply because it was no longer popular—what *PWR* calls the 'zeitgeist interpretation' (ibid., 29)—but because of the changing economic model, the removal of press taxes and the fundamental commercialisation of the press that drove up costs and made it far more difficult for working-class interests and individuals to own popular newspapers. 'Market forces thus accomplished more than the most repressive measures of an aristocratic state' and facilitated the 'progressive transfer of ownership and control of the popular press to wealthy business people' (ibid, 41).

PWR focuses on events after 1830 but this chapter suggests that the founding, in 1821, of the *Manchester Guardian* provides an important, if limited, example from at least a decade before that in that one of the main achievements of the title in the 1820s was to pave the way for 'wealthy business people' to own the press and, in so doing, to squeeze the space for radical titles.[1]

First, as is very well known, the massacre of dozens of ordinary people at Peterloo in 1819 exposed the barbarism of the authorities to a national audience and opened the door to liberal reformers to make a case for piecemeal change and thus to preempt the need to cave in to radical demands for universal suffrage. Indeed, while the 'constitutionalist' wing of the movement gained in confidence following Peterloo, the 'revolutionary' wing, facing sustained repression and internal division, temporarily lost its momentum.

In Manchester, this paved the way for liberal-minded business leaders to agitate for parliamentary reform, religious freedom and, above all, for free trade. People like John Taylor, his good friend and fellow journalist Archibald Prentice and others were part of what was known as the 'Little Circle', a group of Manchester merchants that opposed both the rule of the 'old order' *and* the extension of the franchise to all working people.

Peterloo played a key role in the development of the Circle, convincing its members of the need for a new, constitutionally focused political strategy distinct from that of the radicals. What they lacked at the time was a vehicle that could articulate their values and promote these assemblies—such as a regular newspaper—but the fallout from Peterloo provided precisely this opportunity.

It's important to note that the first instinct of the members of the Little Circle was not to set up their own newspaper but to buy out the liberal *Manchester Gazette*. When this wasn't successful, Taylor secured the necessary capital from his friends in the Manchester business community to launch a newspaper and immediately produced a prospectus designed to publicise its imminent arrival and, more significantly, to secure advertising. The *Guardian*'s current editor, Katharine Viner. describes it as a 'powerful document, and one whose ideals still shape the *Guardian*—a celebration of more people getting educated, of more people engaging in politics, from different walks of life, from poorer communities' (Viner 2017). Yet the prospectus is actually quite cautious in its political orientation, noticeably failing to mention Peterloo nor the government's ongoing repression. Instead, it promised that the newspaper would be committed to 'the promotion of public happiness and the security of popular rights' and that 'it will warmly advocate the cause of reform' without being tied to any particular political party.

In fact, the prospectus makes it clear that the *Manchester Guardian* would be aimed at 'the classes to whom… Advertisements are generally addressed'. Noting that no other Manchester newspaper was fully committed to represent the 'wealth and intelligence of this town,' the prospectus promised that the newspaper would provide comprehensive information about commerce—and about the cotton trade above all.

It is an uncomfortable and unavoidable reality for the *Guardian* that the capital required for its start-up came largely from an industry whose own wealth was intimately bound up with the profits accrued from the slave trade, and the prospectus clearly illustrates that the title was designed to be the house organ of cotton interests. That some of those involved in the paper's founding were active abolitionists does little to change the structural dependence of the title on a source of wealth that directly contradicts its own liberal values or, perhaps more accurately, that reflects the fundamentally compromised history of liberalism itself.

The story of the prospectus, however, shows also that, even at this stage, advertising was a funding mechanism that dangled temptation and deradicalisation at the doors of any so-called progressive title.

Secondly, the *Guardian* did not just open limited space for progressive ideas in a changing England. It actually contributed to and accelerated the demise of the main existing radical newspaper in Manchester, the *Manchester Observer* (very much not to be confused with the present-day title), the top-selling title of the Manchester left and an organiser of the Peterloo protest that, in legend, gave birth to the *Manchester Guardian*. The *Observer* did not lack readers but its support for the more militant wing of the reform movement together with its inability to attract advertising, meant that it was politically and financially vulnerable. The appearance of the *Guardian* only intensified the pressure on the *Observer*, making it harder to attract advertisers and presenting competition that, in the end, it was unable to withstand. The *Manchester Observer* lasted less than a month once the *Guardian* had launched—a foretaste of what was to happen to the Chartist press some 30 years later when market forces and the repeal of press taxes contributed to the demise of a militant press.

The *Guardian* sought alliances not with a militant working-class movement but with liberal business interests that were concentrated in the cotton industry, and pursued an editorial agenda that reflected precisely these interests. Not surprisingly therefore, early chapters about press history in *PWR* barely mention the *Manchester Guardian*. The 'Struggle for a free press' chapter mentions *The Republican*, William Cobbett's *Political Register, Twopenny Trash, Poor Man's Guardian, Voice of the People, Weekly Police Gazette* and of course the *Northern Star*—but *not* the *Manchester Guardian* precisely because it was not a voice for radical social change or working-class insurgency but a mouthpiece for liberal reform.

None of this is ancient history but a valuable reminder of the importance of radical journalism to the ongoing struggles for socialism, democracy and equality and of the importance of radical movements for the possibilities of radical journalism. Crucially, *PWR* reminds us that journalism is not a separate and insulated sphere of professionalised values and craft production from the rest of society but is absolutely intertwined with the patterns of privilege, power and resistance at the heart of societies today and back in the 19th century. Radical journalism has to break free—both in its editorial commitments and its business model—from these patterns.

Power Without Responsibility highlights both the social and economic conditions which shape the media as well as the more subjective political forces that respond to and challenge these conditions. I look forward to the next edition—the ninth—as well as to more spaces for radical journalism that grow out of and stimulate radical movements across the globe.

Note

1 Many of the sources referred to in this chapter are taken from my chapter 'In the Wake of Peterloo: A Radical Account of the Founding of the *Guardian*' in D. Freedman (Ed.) 2021. *Capitalism's Conscience: 200 Years of the Guardian* (pp. 1-18). Pluto Press.

References

Curran, J. and Seaton, J. 2018. *Power Without Responsibility: Press, Broadcasting and the Internet in Britain*, 8th edition. Routledge.

Harrison, S. 1974. *Poor Men's Guardians: A Survey of the Struggles for a Democratic Newspaper Press, 1763–1973*. Lawrence & Wishart.

Hood, S. 1980. *On Television*. Pluto.

Viner, K. 2017. A mission for journalism in a time of crisis. *Guardian*, 16 November. Available at: https://www.theguardian.com/news/2017/nov/16/a-mission-for-journalism-in-a-time-of-crisis.

CHAPTER 24

Writing for Hope: Radical Journalism, Then and Now

Victoria Brittain

How do personal reflections on radical journalism fit into a critical assessment of the book *Power Without Responsibility*? This masterful account of the battles for power and for control over citizens' minds through the media by powerful state and commercial interests over many decades covers a wide field, though not quite this one. The book's importance is well recognised by its several translations as well as by its eight editions. We have to admire the two authors' stamina in producing a ninth edition as the impact of new media technology reaches ever deeper into our lives.

The dramatic and unwelcome new challenges to our profession here in the UK are inescapable but familiar to readers of *Power Without Responsibility*:

- the government has taken a wrecking ball to public service broadcasting with their plans for the BBC and Channel 4;
- the irresponsible Twittersphere (X) hosts billionaires' power projects and attempts to silence journalists;
- state-organised misinformation is on a gigantic scale of unprecedented ambition;
- and journalists face repression, legal cases, prison sentences and assassinations at an accelerating level.

The killing in 2022 of the Al Jazeera journalist Shireen Abu Akleh in Jenin by the Israeli military was one of four killings of female journalists that week: one in Chile and two in Mexico, and one of six Palestinian journalists in the previous two years. At the time of writing, according to the

International Federation of Journalists (2023), 94 Palestinian journalists and media workers have been killed in the war in Gaza.

The most optimistic thing I have to say now is that despite all these well-known dangers and challenges, more than ever young people, particularly I think in the global South, want to become journalists—from a sense of responsibility to tell their people's stories and to fight for accountability. The assassinations referred to above are the terrain these journalists know well.

Existential challenges are so vivid and inescapable in the global South: the very survival of the future of our world under threat from global warming, from nuclear weapons, and from mass death from hunger and thirst. We are increasingly seeing mass movements of desperate people in flight. Media power, mainly in the hands of the political and commercial forces which refuse to face those facts, is a deadly weapon.

Those forces, linked to arms manufacture, fossil fuel exploitation and control over the international mechanisms for peace hammered out after the horrors of World War II, are feeding the new norms of divisions based on ethnicity, religion and sex, and new norms of cruelty and hatred towards the 'other', especially the vulnerable in flight.

So, the title of this chapter, 'Radical Journalism, Then and Now', is certainly a key aspiration for our time and focuses mainly on my own experiences and what radical journalism has meant to me. My early intimations of it came from I.F. Stone's *Weekly* in Washington, *Le Monde Diplomatique* in Paris, and the incomparable Paul Foot in London.

Forty years ago, I did not know Raymond Williams' words that 'to be truly radical is to make hope possible rather than despair convincing' (Williams 1989, 118), but they encapsulate the impetus behind my work, in particular in the *Guardian* in the 1980s. In that Cold War decade, I edited a weekly page in the *Guardian* called 'Third World Review' (TWR). This will feel like pre-history. But, still today, more than thirty years after the page was ended by the then *Guardian* editor Peter Preston, it still happens that I meet new people who immediately associate my name with TWR, and tell me what it meant to them then: hope.

So what was TWR?

It was a full page every Friday featuring writers very largely from the global South. It had been the brainchild of a Pakistani poet, journalist and civil servant, Altaf Gauhar, who persuaded the late Ian Wright, then *Guardian* managing editor, previously foreign editor, that it was a brilliant new venture for the paper into new and cutting-edge territory.

By a great stroke of luck, I had just returned to London after living and working in Saigon, Algiers and most recently for the *Guardian* in East Africa with a wide travelling beat.

TWR was the perfect fit for me—a world I knew. What I knew, from living in the global South, was how right Gauhar was. This was a world where Western economic policies imposed on country after country were bringing catastrophic poverty and social collapse. A large number of intellectuals, writers and academics from these countries were unheard in the West but had a lot to say.

In the 1980s there was an avalanche of coups in 30 countries in the South, 18 of them in Africa, a continent in turmoil. The clandestine proxy wars of the Cold War raged across Southern Africa. The West tagged nationalists as communists, and the CIA gave military support to the white apartheid regime in Pretoria in their proxy wars, assassinations and general destabilisation which ravaged the frontline states which I visited constantly.

TWR was a unique space for writers from the global South to set the agenda and write in a part of the powerful Western media and in a space where other articles, from whichever Southern continent or liberation movement, would have a consistent political tone and context.

A procession of interesting-looking visitors began to arrive in the office to tell me what they wanted to write or see written. They were clever, radical, angry and hopeful—worlds away from the then largely white, male, clubby English world of the *Guardian*. Intellectuals across the South wrote starkly, perhaps too starkly for some of my colleagues who sometimes asked me for 'a right-wing African perspective'.

While right-wing intellectuals were in universities in the West, among TWR's writers were exiles, journalists, poets, novelists, academics, politicians, guerrilla fighters, widows, cartoonists, photographers and political prisoners. In the Raymond Williams sense of being truly radical, they believed their writing made hope possible and was a defence against despair—and TWR readers loved them for it. In later years, some became presidents, others were assassinated.

In today's technological world, it is hard to imagine those days of copy arriving by mail in bulky envelopes, or even often actually brought to me by hand at the paper. In sharp contrast to today's newspaper technology,

TWR's organisation was not just unique but bizarre: edited and sub-edited in London, sent up to Manchester in a parcel driven by courier, made up into a page printed there and driven down again in a parcel by courier. It was a weekly miracle of chaos and serendipity.

Yet behind the pages and their stories lay hours, days, months or even years of direct human communication, long sessions of listening, and tricky unconventional travel. We learned humility and built trust with people who had every reason from their experience not to trust the Western media.

Why was TWR closed down?

The simple answer is because it was too radical and the ideas and their consistency were unwelcome to the powerful. The embassies of the US, apartheid South Africa and Israel, plus powerful British voices (including some inside the paper) constantly criticised the page to the editor. TWR's subjects, and its emphasis on context and history, were a challenge to dominant media agendas. And the pages' writers were a challenge to the assumption that Western journalists were the best reporters on two-thirds of the world's affairs.

So, we lost the battle of TWR's respect for the global South's voices from the outside.

Years later and long-overdue, we now have staff journalists from new and diverse backgrounds including many with powerful individual voices. But, that is a very different situation and a very different impact from being in a regular dedicated section where the reporting and analyses were aspects of a coherent and committed political project.

Today, commercial and political pressures have mainly stripped journalists of the time for listening and the freedom to set our own agendas that the *laissez-faire* days which the *Guardian* of the 1980s gave us in a key decade of ideological struggle, most clearly seen in the global South. All of us now live in a world of many alternatives to the mainstream media, many in the global South. Unlike TWR, those based in the West are mainly focused on UK and US concerns. There are major alternative players in the UK and US which come from a radical perspective, like Open Democracy, or Amy Goodman's *Democracy Now*. Some titles like *The Intercept* and *Counterpunch* have had initial heavyweight funding but finance for radical new platforms is the biggest obstacle to this emerging sector becoming more powerful. There are no easy answers to that.

I would like briefly to mention two small radical media outlets which I am involved in: *Declassified* and *Afrique XX1*. *Declassified* is focused on UK foreign policy and intelligence and was started by Mark Curtis and Matt Kennard in 2019. It covers stories that mainstream media are reluctant or downright unwilling to report on. The second 'void filler' is *Afrique XX1*, a French language website launched in 2021 for specialist writers, academics and journalists on Africa. It is a spin-off idea from the successful *Orient XX1* on the Middle East which now includes articles in Arabic, Persian and English. Many of the writers are writing from their own countries, or about their own countries from exile—much as I tried to do with TWR.

These new experiences underline for me how much today there is real appetite and need for reading and writing radical articles of this quality. The key is articles from journalists who have what we had with TWR: the time and freedom to set our own agendas and to take personal responsibility for reporting, analysing and contextualising truths that are radically inconvenient for the powerful.

This new generation will, I believe, find radical new ways to do this.

References

International Federation of Journalists 2023. Palestine: At Least Fifty Journalists and Media Workers Killed in Gaza, 27 November. Available at: https://www. ifj.org/media-centre/news/detail/category/press-releases/article/palestine-at-least-fifty-one-journalists-and-media-workers-killed-in-gaza
Williams, R. 1989. *Resources of Hope: Culture, Democracy, Socialism.* Verso.

CHAPTER 25

The Black British Press

Omega Douglas

The very existence of some early Black British newspapers, from the *West Indian Gazette* to *The Voice*, was, in and of itself, a radical act. If we take the dictionary definition of 'radical' to mean a belief or expression of 'the belief that there should be great or extreme social or political change', the *West Indian Gazette* (*WIG*), launched in 1958, and *The Voice*, first published in 1982, fit this description. Both rode the wave of calls for social and political change in relation to European colonial and imperial rule and the racism, perpetrated during and post colonialism, which was its lifeblood. That these two commercial newspapers[1] came to exist also poses a challenge to an argument made in *Power Without Responsibility* that advertising did not set the British press free, and that the market 'rendered the press unrepresentative' (Curran and Seaton 2018, 4). This is not to disagree with Curran and Seaton's attack, as they write, on Whig press history and the idea that the story of the British press is one of progress enabled by advertising. Nor is it to agree with some contemporary newspaper editors who assert that advertising and press freedom go hand in hand—a position critiqued by Curran and Seaton (ibid., 5). Rather, this is an invitation to view the role of advertising in relation to the radical press in Britain from an angle not addressed in *PWR*: that of the Black British press.

The market, race and Western journalism

On the one hand, economic logics that inform a market-driven approach to journalism have long obstructed sustained engagement with institutional racism within the journalistic field in Western global economic centres like the UK (Saha 2018; Douglas 2022). Warped economic logics have also been used by some editors and proprietors of mainstream publications as an excuse for their disproportionate representation of white people (Douglas 2019).

On the other hand, the launch of *WIG* and *The Voice* was facilitated, in part, by the market in as much as both newspapers got off the ground with the help of advertising. In this respect, rather than market forces rendering the British press unrepresentative, as Curran and Seaton highlight has been the case since the mid-Victorian period in Britain (Curran and Seaton 2018, 4), the founders of these Black British newspapers worked to harness advertising to carve out representative spaces for people who had never been adequately represented by white-owned British media.

Writing self into the land

The pioneering Claudia Jones, founder of the Notting Hill Carnival, who arrived in the UK from Trinidad via the US in 1955,[2] launched *WIG* with the masthead 'Afro-Asian Caribbean [peoples]' (Hinds 2008). As Courtman (2021) highlights, Jones put into practice what Raymond Williams describes in his 1958 essay 'Culture is Ordinary', by channelling her energy into cultural activism to celebrate the culture of those excluded from centres of power. This included establishing *WIG* so that the African, Asian and Caribbean diaspora in Britain had a vehicle for 'writing themselves into the land' (Williams 2013, 2). Both the carnival and *WIG* encapsulated Jones's belief that 'a people's art is the genesis of their freedom' (Frazer-Carroll 2020).

The aim of *WIG*, at a time when political Blackness was embraced by some people of colour as a strategically essentialist term to organise around in a unified fight against racism, was to contribute to the struggle for the rights of people from Africa, Asia and the Caribbean. Jones was a committed campaigner, incarcerated in the US for her involvement with the American Communist Party, and her activism was reflected in *WIG*'s editorial content. From supportive coverage of freedom fighters like Nelson Mandela, 'labelled by the British national broadsheets as [...] terrorists' (Hinds 2008, 95), to the celebration of Castro's revolution, *WIG* supported independence struggles around the world. In Britain, it was the only 'voice of the black community between 1958 and 1965, [...] sold for sixpence (2.5p) and it accepted what advertisements came its way' (Hinds 2008, 89–90). Jones, who said 'people without a voice were like lambs to the slaughter' (Frazer-Carroll 2020), did not draw a salary. Although *WIG* got some advertising from businesses that had a large Black customer base, including the Grimaldi-Siosa Line whose ships carried passengers between the Caribbean and the UK from 1948 to the mid-1960s (Hinds 2008), the newspaper struggled financially. It closed shortly after Jones's death in 1964, when she was just 49.

While *WIG* emphasised the regions of the world that its target audience emigrated to Britain from, *The Voice*, whose masthead used the words Black and Britain,[3] equated Blackness with Britishness in a way no other media platform had and at a time when the words 'Black' *and* 'British' were perceived by many as mutually exclusive.

Launched in 1982 in the aftermath of uprisings across England, from St Pauls to Brixton, which occurred in response to systemic racism, particularly police treatment of Black people,[4] *The Voice* contributed to a new imagining of Black Britain. At a time when levels of overt racism meant many Black people rejected any sense that they were British, *The Voice* offered a space for negotiating Black British identities.

As a former *Voice* journalist, I would not describe the newspaper as consistently producing radical journalism in terms of its content. Unlike Claudia Jones, *The Voice's* founder, Val McCalla, was an entrepreneur rather than a selfless campaigner. However, *The Voice* did position itself as a key platform in the struggle against racism. Its first front page featured a story about a Black London family who were being targeted by a racist gang. It was also the first newspaper to interview the family of Colin Roach, a 21-year-old Black man who died in suspicious circumstances in Stoke Newington Police Station (Ruddock 2018). *The Voice* continued to highlight racial injustice at a time when there was rarely, if any, mainstream news coverage of racism in Britain. That was as radical as the newspaper's small but significant symbolic acts like equating Blackness with Britishness and the fact that *The Voice*, perhaps unwittingly, contributed to affecting systemic change within white-dominated media. It did so by providing a training ground for many talented Black journalists during an era when it was nigh-on impossible to get a permanent position, let alone your first journalism job, in the mainstream press if you weren't white and middle or upper class. Lots of journalists who left *The Voice*, such as Joseph Harker[5] and Afua Hirsch, went on to agitate for change in the media and other sectors, so that people of colour can enjoy that simple, but powerful thing: to be able to turn on our televisions, read magazines and newspapers, and feel more adequately represented.

But of course a single newspaper cannot speak to the limitless identities that make up a nation nor segments of it, and many Black people, particularly in later years, did not identify with *The Voice*. Class played a role in whether Black Britons considered themselves represented by *The Voice*, which published in tabloid format in line with other newspapers aimed at working-class audiences, of which Black Britons predominantly formed a part in the 1980s. That has shifted over the years, but race and class continue to intersect in Britain, and we don't pay enough attention to that intersection, with the term 'working-class' typically associated with white Britons (Leeds 2019). That *The Voice*, initially at least, offered a space for the voices of working-class Black Britons to be heard, was also pretty radical. It remains so in an era where, as the Grenfell Tower tragedy showed us, the voices of working-class people of colour in Britain often continue to be ignored (Townsend 2020).

The role of advertising

Crucially, *The Voice* would not have launched and sustained itself without advertising. The newspaper capitalised on a moment when certain advertisers were keen to get behind Black causes. Lots of the newspaper's advertising came from public sector jobs, due to the push from councils to recruit Black staff after the 1980s uprisings, and the systemic racism the uprisings forced a degree of wider public recognition of (Webber 2016).

Barclays Bank also loaned *The Voice* start-up capital. No doubt keen to offset negative publicity the bank received due to doing business in apartheid-era South Africa, the logics informing Barclays' move are comparable to the 'racial capitalism' (Leong 2013) operationalised by some white-owned companies that have sought to financially benefit from the Black Lives Matter movement (Bokat-Lindell 2020). This involves displays of apparent solidarity with the movement to boost a brand's social and economic value, without addressing the structural racism within their own organisations.

Despite advertising being integral to its success, *The Voice* was also political whilst being independent of government just like, as Curran and Seaton highlight, early radical British papers. More recent radical publications, like

Gal-Dem,[6] which launched in 2015 to cater to people of colour who remain mis- and underrepresented in mainstream British journalism, are also reliant on advertising (Kelly 2020) and other commercial ventures like brand partnerships. Thus, rather than market forces rendering the British press unrepresentative, for those who have, and continue to be, inadequately represented by the dominant British press, advertising, though limited and hard-won, has helped subsidise vital forms of radical British journalism.

Notes

1 Before the *West Indian Gazette* was published, Harold Moody, a Jamaican doctor who arrived in England to study medicine in 1904, founded the League of Coloured Peoples (LCP), a Black British civil rights organisation, in 1931. Two years later, he launched *The Keys*, a journal that represented the interests of the LCP. It was focused on promoting the rights of Black people in Britain and the then British Empire, as well as highlighting inequality experienced by people of colour around the world—from South Africa to Australia. The LCP, which was dissolved in 1951, four years after Moody's death, also published pamphlets and had letters published in national British newspapers (Staveley-Wadham 2021). Earlier publications by Black people in Britain include 19th-century abolitionist literature and 18th-century writing by people of African heritage, such as Ottobah Cugoano and Olaudah Equiano, who recounted the horrors of their lived experience as slaves.

2 Jones was deported to Britain (where she was a 'subject' as Trinidad was then part of the British empire) from the US due to her intersectional politics. Before the term 'intersectionality' (Crenshaw 1991) was coined, Jones recognised what Sandra Courtman describes as 'the need to integrate, theoretically and practically, the communist fight against capitalist exploitation with anti-racist and anti-sexist discourses' (Courtman 2021).

3 The newspaper's first masthead was 'London's First Black Newspaper'. Soon after it branded itself 'Britain's Best Black Newspaper'.

4 This included via the Sus law, which enabled the police to stop and search anyone they merely suspected may be planning to commit a crime. The law was disproportionately used to target Black men who could be arrested for simply walking down the street. In April 1981, just before the Brixton uprising, during what was termed 'Operation Swamp', the police stopped over 1,000 Black people in Brixton using Sus.

5 Harker is now the *Guardian's* Senior Editor for Diversity and Development.

6 Unfortunately, *Gal-Dem* closed in spring 2023 due to financial difficulties.

References

Bokat-Lindell, S. 2020. Opinion: Are Black Lives What Really Matter to Companies?. *New York Times*, 23 June. Available at: https://www.nytimes.com/2020/06/23/opinion/black-lives-matter-brands.html

Courtman, S. 2021. *Claudia Jones' rebel heart | The British Library*. Available at: https://www.bl.uk/windrush/articles/claudia-jones-rebel-heart

Crenshaw, K. W. 1991. Mapping the Margins: Intersectionality, Identity Politics, and Violence against Women of Color. *Stanford Law Review*, 43(6), 1241–99.

Curran, J. and Seaton, J. 2018. *Power Without Responsibility: Press, Broadcasting and the Internet in Britain*, 8th edition. Routledge.

Douglas, O. 2019. *Backstories / Black Stories: Black Journalists, INGOs and the Racial Politics of Representing Sub-Saharan Africa in Mainstream UK News Media*. Doctoral thesis, Goldsmiths, University of London. Available at: http://research.gold.ac.uk/26352/

Douglas, O. 2022. The Media Diversity and Inclusion Paradox: Experiences of Black and Brown Journalists in Mainstream British News Institutions. *Journalism*, 23(10), 2096–2113. https://doi.org/10.1177/14648849211001778

Frazer-Carroll, M. 2020. *The Runnymede Trust | Black history legacies: Claudia Jones*. Available at: https://www.runnymedetrust.org//blog/black-history-legacies-claudia-jones.

Hinds, D. 2008. The West Indian Gazette: Claudia Jones and the Black Press in Britain. *Race & Class*, 50(1), 88–97. https://doi.org/10.1177/0306396808050 0010602

Kelly, T. 2020. 'A Bittersweet Moment': How Gal-dem Launched Membership Amid Black Lives Matter protests and COVID-19', *Poynter*, 24 September. Available at: https://www.poynter.org/reporting-editing/2020/a-bittersweet-moment-how-gal-dem-launched-membership-amid-black-lives-matter-protests-and-covid-19/

Leong, N. 2013. Racial Capitalism. *Harvard Law Review*, 126(8), 2151–2226.

Ruddock, G. 2018. *Voice 35 Years: Standing Up for What We Believe | The Voice Online*. Available at: https://archive.voice-online.co.uk/article/voice-35-years-standing-what-we-believe.

Saha, A. 2018. *Race and the Cultural Industries*. Polity Press.

Staveley-Wadham, R. 2021. *Unlocking Black British History: An Introduction to 'The Keys' Journal*. Available at: https://blog.britishnewspaperarchive.co.uk/2021/09/29/unlocking-black-british-history-an-introduction-to-the-keys-journal/

Townsend, M. 2020. Grenfell Families Want Inquiry To Look at Role of 'Race and Class' in Tragedy. *The Observer*, 26 July. Available at: https://www.theguardian.com/uk-news/2020/jul/26/grenfell-families-want-inquiry-to-look-at-role-of-race-and-class-in-tragedy

University of Leeds 2019. Busting the Myth of the 'White Working Class'. Available at: https://www.leeds.ac.uk/news-society-politics/news/article/4462/busting-the-myth-of-the-white-working-class

Webber, E. 2016. The rise and fall of the GLC. *BBC News*, 31 March. Available at: https://www.bbc.com/news/uk-england-london-35716693

Williams, R. 2013. *Raymond Williams on Culture and Society: Essential Writings*. 1st edition. J. McGuigan (Ed.). Sage Publications.

Part VI
Afterword

CHAPTER 26

Power Without Responsibility: Looking Back

James Curran

Power Without Responsibility happened fortuitously. I was asked by a senior politician to rewrite his book on contemporary media which had failed to find a publisher. I involved Jean Seaton in the rewrite, and we both then realised that the book was unsalvageable.[1] Why not, Jean suggested, write a book that we wanted to write? The book turned out to be *Power Without Responsibility* (*PWR*).

Multiple 'midwives' assisted its birth. The first was the Cambridge Labour historian, Henry Pelling, who was my PhD supervisor and suggested British press history as the subject of my research because 'not much has been done on the subject'. The second was Hugh Cudlipp, then Chairman of the Mirror Group (IPC), who offered me a job. My response was that I would rather have a research grant. He wrote a cheque which enabled me to extend my research on press history and secure a temporary Research Fellowship at the Open University. The third midwife was another Welshman, Raymond Williams, who urged a senior publishing executive (and his former student) to commission *PWR* as a trade book. Without Williams' patronage, I doubt whether two obscure polytechnic lecturers would have got a mass paperback commission.

In my case, the book was shaped by two contradictory influences. I had a privileged private school education and had been wonderfully well taught in one-to-one tutorials at Trinity College, Cambridge. These could be brutal. The historian Sir John Elliott said to me: 'Curran, you speak in an interesting way but you are very dull when you write. You must fix this.' This was good advice. But nearly all the teachers at my schools and the academics I came across as an undergraduate were Conservatives. Happily,

I went to a second university in the form of the Huntingdonshire Labour Party. Its members were overwhelmingly working class and (in Labour Party terms) right-wing. They came—sometimes grudgingly—to accept and educate me. For my part, I have never met a group of people I admired and liked more than them.

The sense of mission I obtained from them gave me courage. The essays I wrote which paved the way to *PWR* encountered a lot of flak. The leading American historian Stephen Koss refused to meet me on the grounds that he might be put in the 'compromised position' of having to shake my hand. The distinguished Stanford University communications professor, Steven Chaffee, came up to me at a conference and said that an essay I had just published was 'rubbish'. At the time I had no idea who he was, said that I was sure that he was right and asked politely whether he had seen any interesting sights in London. Rather more intimidatingly, Professor Sir Brian Harrison wrote a rebuttal of my work in a clever, scholarly and courteous essay.[2]

These responses were prompted by my attack on the orthodox interpretation of British press history as a story of progress in which newspapers became free from government and represented public opinion. My counter-argument was that market censorship had succeeded where state repression had failed in stifling radical journalism. As a consequence, the newspapers that emerged free of state control tended to serve the interests of power and privilege.

Radical newspapers built a mass readership between 1830 and 1850 despite attempts to suppress them through legal prosecution and press taxes designed to price newspapers beyond the reach of the working class. Many of these papers attacked the monarchy and aristocracy, developed a more left-wing critique of an undemocratic, capitalist society, campaigned for radical change and conferred status on left-wing activists. But in the second half of the 19th century, the radical press was eclipsed by more centrist and right-wing papers. When the Labour Party made a breakthrough in the 1918 general election, it did not have the support of a single national daily.

There were several causes of this transformation. Among the most important were the structural changes that took place in the press industry between 1850 and 1920. The rise in the capital and operating costs of newspapers led to a transfer of press ownership to the wealthy, while increased dependence on advertising (due to the lowering of cover prices) undermined radical publications because advertisers discriminated against them.

This argument is qualified in relation to the 20th century because the functioning of the newspaper market changed. Advertising discrimination against left publications declined due to the development of more data-based advertising selection and the increased spending power of the working class, making them more attractive to advertisers. Newsprint rationing during World War II freed the press from economic constraints and contributed to the revival of left journalism at a time of wartime radicalisation. In the 1960s and 1970s, some press owners devolved decision-making, enabling the emergence of journalist-run newspapers like the *Sunday Times* under Harold Evans' editorship.

But press ownership remained highly concentrated. A new generation of proprietors asserted centralised control of the press from the late 1970s onwards. They formed an alliance with New Right politicians and helped to remake Britain as a more unequal and fearful society. Although newspaper circulation declined, the press influenced television and also social media. National popular papers also pursued a successful anti-competition strategy by giving away their online content free. This undermined digital-born rivals if they charged a subscription, and forced up the launch costs of new news websites if they matched this free offer.

What happened in the press is very different from British broadcasting. Jean Seaton traces in *PWR* the evolution of the BBC from being the mouthpiece of government, as in the 1926 General Strike, to becoming increasingly independent—a shift marked by the BBC's defiance of government bullying during the 1956 Suez War. She also documents how broadcasters built a mass audience and adapted in stages to the diversity of public demand through the restructuring of radio channels in the 1940s and 1960s, the introduction of regulated commercial television in 1955 and the advent of Channel 4 in 1982. Implicitly she portrays the 1960s as the high point of public service television when new kinds of drama, documentaries and entertainment were introduced. The subsequent period was characterised by increasing caution, managerialism and latterly budget cuts in the BBC.

Nevertheless, the overall conclusion of her history is that public service broadcasting contributed to progress in informing, educating and entertaining the nation. It has in her phrase—cited several times in this book—an 'imperfect beauty' which acknowledges its flaws but asserts its overall achievement and contribution to the public good. And because public service broadcasting is both popular and valued in Britain, it has survived in the neoliberal age.

The book thus draws a sharp contrast between public service broadcasting which, despite some limitations, has enriched the nation, and a predominantly right-wing national press which in the last thirty years has harried the poor, campaigned against migrants, stigmatised Muslims and promoted law and order politics with an undertow of racism.

Later editions have traced the history of the internet. They contrast the pioneer days of the internet, when it was shaped by the cooperative values of science, countercultural experiment and a public service tradition that created the World Wide Web, with its subsequent hyper-commercialisation and capture by tech giants. But there was a pushback in the form of cooperative ventures like Wikipedia and user-generated sites that replicated the DIY tradition of the pioneer internet. The rise of social media has advanced the democratisation of communication, although Jean Seaton emphasises that they have also spread disinformation and fostered polarisation.

Something should be said about how we wrote and revised *PWR*. The first edition took four years to research and write. We found that we disagreed on some things even though we are both social democrats. Differences were resolved by writing separate chapters and clearly specifying their authorship in the table of contents. It also helped that we like each other and are part of overlapping social networks. Jean Seaton's first husband Ben Pimlott (who died) was my closest school friend and I and my wife are deeply attached to her second husband, David Loyn. Even so, relations were not always warm in the writing of the first edition. 'James Curran,' Jean wrote (Curran and Seaton 1981, 289), 'does not share any of Jean Seaton's reservations about the writers discussed in this part of the chapter.' The word 'any', implying a totally uncritical response on my part (not true), conveys the vexation that Jean must have felt at the time.

I am grateful to the people who have commented—both critically and favourably—on *PWR* and have read with deep interest how its themes have been explored outside Britain. I also have criticisms of the book. In its early editions, the history of the press was too narrowly materialist, although in later editions I offer a broader contextualisation of the development of the press. My approach has shifted still further. In my latest book (Curran and Redden 2024), I advance a conjunctural perspective of the media as being shaped by the changing balance of social forces and ideas in society. A further limitation is that while *PWR* gives attention to British media policy—pointing to its contradictions and surveying the different approaches to media reform—it has never pinned down how the internet and AI should be regulated in the public interest.

But the book has been in print for over forty years. When it first came out, it connected to the zeitgeist of the time and was for a time top of the independent bookshops' bestseller list (compiled by *City Limits*). It has morphed into being a polemical textbook used in schools and universities. Indeed, in a mysterious way, it seems to have attracted more academic attention in recent years. Between the writing of the eighth and ninth editions, approximately a thousand additional publications cited *Power Without Responsibility*.[3]

Revising and updating *PWR* (including the writing of new chapters) has kept the book current. But this is a demanding process requiring energy and commitment. 'The next edition, due to be published in 2025, will be the last'.

Notes

1 Despite being a government minister and subsequently a life peer, he was without self-importance. He remained friendly and charming when we moved on.

2 Brian Harrison presented a liberal pluralist account of press history in his essay 'Press and pressure group in modern Britain' in J. Shattock and M. Wolff (Eds.) 1982. *The Victorian Periodical Press.* University of Toronto Press. This argument worked better for periodicals (the focus of his analysis) than for national newspapers. Even so, I incorporated his critique as a qualification in later editions.

3 When we finished writing the eighth edition in 2017, Google Scholar recorded 1,600 citations of all editions of *PWR*: in December 2023, this had risen to 2,567. This increase may be due to the book winning an international award (the International Communication Association Fellows Book Award) in 2019 or perhaps a change in the way Google Scholar tabulates citations.

References

Curran, J. and Seaton, J. 1981. *Power Without Responsibility: The Press and Broadcasting in Britain.* Fontana.

Curran, J. and Redden, J. 2024. *Understanding Media: Communication, Power and Social Change.* Pelican.

CHAPTER 27

The Birth of *Power Without Responsibility*

Jean Seaton

The newspapers attacking me are not newspapers in the ordinary sense. They are engines of propaganda for the constantly changing policies, desires, personal vices, personal likes and dislikes of the two men. What are their methods? Their methods are direct falsehoods, misrepresentation, half-truths, the alteration of the speaker's meaning by publishing a sentence apart from the context... What the proprietorship of these papers is aiming at is power, and power without responsibility—the prerogative of the harlot throughout the ages. (Quoted in Middlemass and Barnes 1963, 121)

This was Stanley Baldwin, the Conservative Prime Minister, speaking of press barons in 1936. His cousin Rudyard Kipling had suggested the line to him. Kipling had first described the press as having 'power without responsibility' in a short story, 'The Village that Voted the Earth was Flat' (Kipling, n.d.) on how elections were stolen by the press in 1916. Ben Pimlott gave us the title.

Power Without Responsibility (PWR) was born out of opportunity, ambition, a bustling sense that things should be better, and a little frustration.

We knew that the media made the weather for politics, helped form mores and manners for better or worse, could be a creative expression of society as well as, at times, instruments of unseen, unaccountable influence. We thought there should be more of a struggle over the use of all this power. We wanted to interrogate the structures that made this happen—who owned, controlled and regulated this important lever of democracy. In the world we came from, when we started on this road fifty years ago, the academy rarely engaged with policymaking. We were part of a wave coming from different academic backgrounds who saw 'the media' as important.

Curran would become a founding figure in creating media studies as a discipline, but at the time we had a blithe disregard for academic disciplinary boundaries. Politics, history, social science, surveys, evidence, ideas, novels—anything that was interesting and helped understand the media was useful. History was key: how had things got how they were? History may never repeat itself, nevertheless it has rhythms.

We wanted to be different, to make a difference, and on the way to the book we contributed to a 1974 Labour Party policy document, called *The People and the Media* (Labour Party 1974). Curran had strong trade union roots, stood as a Labour candidate and later edited the Labour Party magazine *New Socialist*. Looking back, frankly, our idea of policy making was to write down an ideal state of affairs and assume that someone else (a magic policy fairy?) would make it happen. It took time to understand campaigning but also the complexity and cunning of effective policy: although we also wanted everyone to be interested in it. The underside of how things get made was our topic.

Curran brought original historical research on the radical 19th-century press to the project. It overturned conventional accounts and prefigured Jürgen Habermas's work (not translated into English until 1989) on democratic culture and the 'public sphere' in the 18th century (Habermas 1989). Unusually in Britain, Curran also had professional experience in commercial social survey research. As a student at Cambridge he supplemented his grant by doing surveys (working with the first commercially viable computers). His first commission was for a company called Regent Petrol. His work showed that advertising had led to consumers attaching different qualities to different brands—one brand devoted to people who wanted petrol to 'look after' their car, another to 'nurse it', or make it go faster, or further. It was a demonstration that advertising could create reality, since cynical petrol executives told him that there was no difference between brands. Another survey found that readers of the *Financial Times* valued it because it made them feel part of a technical elite. But they also wanted more about culture and profiles of business leaders: the beginning of up-market *FT*-flavoured fun. The *FT* loved the report because it meant they could reshape the paper without losing their niche as a prestige purchase.

This background gave Curran the capacity to assess evidence with a professional eye. He could discriminate between what was important and what was obfuscating in the American empirical quantification of media effects. This imbued all the work that followed with Curran's original, witty suspicion and authority. He works deductively: he knows what the argument will be. One might put his work in the company of historians like E. P. Thompson, whose book, *The Making of the English Working Class* (Thompson 1968), was a seminal text for many historians of that generation; or a historian like Robert Darnton, who drew on popular songs, discussions, pornography and radical printing to explain how the French Revolution gathered energy and indeed the move from equality, fraternity and hope towards extreme violence (Darnton 1979, 1984). Historians had been working on everyday life and working-class culture two decades before reception studies in the media took off. And during its different editions, *PWR* has necessarily been a product of the ideas, politics and culture of its time. But it was also the product of a publishing breakthrough (Curran had the contract) to write a book whose imperative was to be scholarly but clear. Clarity and simplicity are philosophical and political positions we share.

When he started, Curran was determined to reveal how important alternative press voices were excluded from access to audiences: this work fed straight into a series of campaigns focused on altering the conditions of entry to media markets. He wanted to explain how the commercial structures of ownership and advertising distorted the range of people, points of view and kinds of evidence that could secure public attention. For Seaton, beginning at a time when there were only three TV channels, the book started with how the values and practice of publicly owned, public service broadcasting could be positive, and what threatened that ecosystem. Curran thought more of ownership, I thought more of regulation. What makes the difference between Fox News, knowingly polluting reality for ratings (and profit) in the USA, and Sky News in the UK, a perfectly serious news channel, once both owned by Murdoch? One answer is regulation.

Earlier, I had been as ferociously diligent as anyone in attempting to follow the superficially appealing dogmatisms of the moment. We were very serious about our Marxism, although at least viscerally opposed to Stalinism. We read Antonio Gramsci on the Party and Hans Magnus Enzenberger on the radicalism of the photocopier. Anthony Barnett, later the founder of Open Democracy, was an important influence when he arrived at Leicester University, where I was an undergraduate.[1]

Retrospectively, the *New Left Review* (at the heart of this strand of the left) was like an exclusive cult you could not join, with superior gurus. It was agreed that the problem with the United Kingdom was that it had not had a 'proper revolution' and lacked 'proper theory'. These were truths universally acknowledged by people who had a shaky idea of the actual foundations of British democracy in 1688. The idea of 'revolution' was worshipped but it was a shameful sin to question what might happen the next day. Later there was a lower middle-class riposte to this in the shape of dedication to the work of Louis Althusser. These were the theory years: as if the world would alter in the face of the 'correct' theory. This strand of ideas and some of the groups around it led directly to the deadly impenetrable dogma and jargon of Judith Butler, with the simplistic view that there is no such thing as an author, a body, intention, or indeed facts (only what readers and consumers make of things) and a bizarre relativistic certitude. This is a world where the only certainty is that everything is relative: a logical impossibility.

What shifted from a search for orthodoxy to potentially malleable uncertainty—and as a consequence the possibility of doing something to help positive change? Sociology offered another more dynamic view. It was Durkheim who had the grand idea that 'the totality of the beliefs and sentiments common to the average citizens of the same society formed a determinate system which has its own life' (Durkheim 1933, 79). This was not the power of ideas in a mob (history was to be better at that) but it was useful. Max Weber's *Politics as a Vocation* (1919) and the idea of the *development* of politics and change which was quite different from the Marxist succession of stages following each other with machine-like inevitability. Unfashionably, I turned to J. S. Mill. Freedom of speech for Mill was not an opportunity to win but more like a human relationship in a George Eliot novel, for example in *Daniel Deronda*, a thing that might flourish or wither, so all sides of the argument had a chance to change, and indeed grow and expand the sympathy of all. This brought development and generosity as dynamic opportunities into how we might see the media and how they could enrich as well as diminish collective and personal lives.

Naturally I was a feminist. Anyone who had roneoed (then the new cheap way of printing radical magazines for men to pontificate in—even if you liked the men) would be. Feminism, like the left, collapsed into schisms but was exhilarating. The (no doubt rather weak) version of it that shaped *PWR*, which appears bizarre now, meant that I never saw any subject—wars, policy, journalism, defence reviews, politics, or the origins of early music in the BBC as off limits. We take it for granted in today's world where the editors of the *Economist, Financial Times*, the *Guardian*, and the boss of Channel 4 are all women and that women can be interested in anything. That was not so true then.

Another odd, formative experience for me was interviewing people in Portugal during its 1974–1975 revolution. The topsy-turvy world of a real revolution showed everything in flux. After the quite nasty authoritarian Caetano regime fell in 1974, following a revolt in the Portuguese colonies, there was a left-wing, pro-democratic military coup. Support for the Communists, hardline orthodox Stalinists, but brave resistors, unexpectedly collapsed in the first elections. America decided to trust the revolution. I had been taught by the brilliant, maverick Portuguese exile Herminio Martins,[2] who was both elated and galvanised by and sardonically distrustful of much of what was happening, and that was a useful corrective. What emerged was not an ideology-driven utopia, and certainly not the terrifying Soviet model, but something that served the Portuguese people far better. Yet as it unfolded it seemed to need *both* the Annales School analysis, being the product of great waves of historical change, as well as being a lesson in the impact of political leadership.

Ben Pimlott, Curran's oldest friend, later my husband, was transformative. Pimlott was a historian, an activist in Labour politics and Chair of the Fabians. He reformulated Labour's idea of what mattered and more widely made the case for Labour ideas in a series of biographies that always started with the unfashionable: Hugh Dalton and Harold Wilson were both despised by parts of the Labour movement when he turned his attention to them. Pimlott brought the interplay of character, research and vision that combine to make progressive politics effective.

Of course, there was Asa Briggs's magnificent history of the BBC (who I later succeeded as official historian of the BBC after his long tenure writing the first six volumes of *The History of Broadcasting in the United Kingdom*). Briggs was resentful that this work was never considered a fitting subject for history by Oxford and Cambridge and some historians still argue that he should have stayed with 'proper' 19th-century history (Taylor 2014). Yet Briggs explored the inner machinery of an institution; he appreciated the 'high politics' of broadcasting and the great popular side of it as well. His work was like a door opening to a new way of exploring the media. A wonder of research, it also showed how vital institutions are and yet in Briggs's volumes there is an inevitability in the process of becoming the BBC. I, on the other hand, saw it as a more precarious institution.

An aspect of all this new work was that it was about Britain. In something of a rebellion away from the abstract, international theory years, we worried about the polity we lived in. Everybody lives locally—it is not parochial to investigate it. Journalism and reporting are not merely (although they are) constructs: at their best, awkward reporters find out things we need to know. Journalism, rather more than academic criticism, is an everyday exercise of moral discrimination with consequences. This all added up to a project of the shifting, sadly often untethered, nature of history as it happens. A proper investigation of history happens when things can be seen that are not as they first seemed. It shed a light on what made Britain as it changed. It seemed rather unfashionable at the time, but it is what drove our work. It was never that we thought audiences, the public, citizens could be simply duped. But it was surely right to ask what shaped their understanding of events and the world. Oddly, this localism provided a model for other local explorations. The book, paradoxically, was internationalist because it was particular and located in a specific context: it was the urge to understand something particular that offered a model for other investigations.

The answers were knotty. Yet the problems have got worse. Advertising on TV and the press (which we understood well) was a pale ancestor to the rapacious viral advertising that has now reshaped the world: the effects are similar but scaled up monstrously. As it turns out, public policy—especially as in the case of the internet, search engines and social media—has completely failed to manage the companies and forces that determine the new information space. As a consequence, software engineers have redesigned societies and politics in the interests of profit or manipulation. These platforms have all had positive effects, but they have not been managed in the public collective interest. In 2024 more people are about to vote than have ever voted before and yet these elections and the conventions that have emerged may well be shattered by AI that we are struggling to comprehend let alone regulate. Behaviour can be bought and altered in a way that has not been possible before. It is not clear that the sociology that showed that opinion was based in social structure has anything to say to a social structure that had disappeared *inside* the media: like Jonah in the whale. As Martin Moore put it in his brilliant and prescient book, *Democracy Hacked*, 'Our laws don't cover what is happening and our politicians don't understand it' (Moore 2018). I have worked closely with Moore at the Media Standards Trust and in growing the Orwell Foundation.

Yet through its many editions, the book rejected the passivity and the Olympian disdain that characterised academic and much left-wing thinking about the grubby politics of altering things: for the better, not perfectly or ideologically. The journey was an attempt, however faulty, to understand things, contexts, people, and history. It has not always been a success—we missed so many things, called some out wrongly, but it was important to try. The media shape how we see the world and what we concentrate on; what 'they' are has altered dramatically but they did when we started, and they do so even more now.

We try to see things as they are and fail. But for a critical and contrary book, *PWR* was—and remains—peculiarly positive. It is, after all, a book concerned with encouraging everyone to understand better and above all to take responsibility and care.

Notes

1 Barnett arrived to work with Norbert Elias (whose seminal *The Civilizing Process* was not translated until far later, but who was personally a counterweight to all of this).

2 Herminio Martins wrote widely on theory and later became a prominent analyst of Brazil: his last book, *The Technocene: Reflections on Bodies, Minds, and Markets* (2018, Athene Press), has a collection of many of his grand and ranging essays.

References

Darnton, R. 1979. *The Business of the Enlightenment*. Harvard University Press.

Darnton, R. 1984. *The Great Cat Massacre and Other Episodes in French Cultural History*. Basic Books.

Durkheim, E. 1933. *The Division of Labour in Society*. Free Press.

Habermas, J. 1989. *The Structural Transformation of the Public Sphere: An Inquiry into a Category of Bourgeois Society*. Polity Press.

Kipling, R. (no date). The Village that Voted that the World was Flat. https://www.kiplingsociety.co.uk/readers-guide/rg_villagevoted1.htm

Labour Party 1974. *The People and the Media*. Labour Party.

Middlemass, K. and Barnes, J. 1963. *Stanley Baldwin*. Oxford University Press.

Moore, M. 2018. *Democracy Hacked*. Simon & Schuster.

Taylor, M. (Ed.) 2014. *The Age of Asa: Lord Briggs, Public Life and History in Britain Since 1945*. Oxford University Press.

Thompson, E. P. 1968. *The Making of the English Working Class*. Pelican.

ABOUT THE CONTRIBUTORS

Afonso de Albuquerque is Professor at the Communication Studies Program at Fluminense Federal University, Brazil. He is the coordinator of the National Institute of Science and Technology – Informational Disputes and Sovereignty project. His research interests include journalism, political communication and comparative studies in communication.

Patrick Barwise is Emeritus Professor of Management and Marketing at London Business School, Chairman of the Archive of Market and Social Research and former Chairman of *Which?*. He has published on a wide range of topics in management, marketing and media. His 1988 book *Television and its Audience*, co-authored with Andrew Ehrenberg, has never been out of print. His latest book, *The War Against the BBC*, co-authored with Peter York, was published by Penguin in 2020.

Victoria Brittain has lived and worked as a journalist in Washington, Saigon, Algiers, Nairobi and London. She worked at the *Guardian* for 25 years as a foreign correspondent and as a foreign desk editor in London. She has also worked with many French and US publications. She has written several books about Africa during the end of the Cold War, about Guantanamo Bay and the impact of the war on terror on women, and most recently a study of the work of Palestinian film director Mai Masri.

James Curran is Professor of Communications at Goldsmiths, University of London. His authored books include *Media and Power* (Routledge 2002), *Media and Democracy* (2011), *Understanding Media: Communication, Power and Social Change* (with Joanna Redden) (2024) and *Power Without Responsibility* (with Jean Seaton) 9th edition (2024). His co-edited books include *De-Westernising Media Studies* (2000) and *Media and Society*, 6th edition (Bloomsbury Academic, 2019). He has been a Visiting

Professor at the Universities of California, Oslo, Stockholm, Stanford and Pennsylvania.

Otávio Daros is Postdoctoral Researcher at the School of Communications, Arts and Design at the Pontifical Catholic University of Rio Grande do Sul (PUCRS). In addition to holding a dual PhD at Nottingham Trent University, he was a Guest Researcher in the communication history divisions at the University of Bremen and the Free University of Berlin. He is the author of the book *Writing Journalism History: The Press and Academia in Brazil* (Routledge, 2024).

Aeron Davis is Professor of Political Communication and Programme Director of the Bachelor and Masters Programmes of Communication at Victoria University of Wellington, New Zealand. He was previously at the Department of Media, Communication and Cultural Studies at Goldsmiths, University of London (2006–20) where he had been Professor of Political Communication, Co-head of Department and Co-director of Goldsmiths Political Economy Research Centre (PERC). He is the author or editor of ten books and over 70 other publications in journals, edited collections and news media including, most recently, a second edition of *Political Communication: An Introduction for Crisis Times* (2024).

Karen Donders is Director of Public Value, Talent and Organization at Flemish public broadcaster VRT and is member of its Board of Directors. She is Associate Professor at the Vrije Universiteit Brussel and affiliated member of research group imec-SMIT.

Omega Douglas is Lecturer in the Media, Communications and Cultural Studies Department at Goldsmiths, University of London, where she convenes the BA in Journalism. She is co-author of *Journalism, Culture and Society* (Routledge, 2023), and is currently working on another book for Routledge: *The Racial Dynamics of Reporting Africa: Colonial and Decolonial Practices in Mainstream Western News*. Her research interests are race, representation, media diversity and the role of diasporic communities, as well as international institutions, such as INGOs, in global communications. Prior to working in academia, she practised as a journalist and editor for various British media organisations.

Natalie Fenton is Professor of Media and Communications at Goldsmiths, University of London where she is also Co-director of the Centre for the Study of Global Media and Democracy. She was Vice-chair of the board of the campaign group Hacked Off for seven years and a founding member and former Chair of the UK Media Reform Coalition. She is also on the Board of Declassified UK, an investigative journalism website for in-depth analysis on British foreign policy. Her latest books include *Media, Democracy and Social Change: Re-imagining Political Communications,* co-authored with Des Freedman, Gholam Khiabany and Aeron Davis (2020), *The Media Manifesto* with Des Freedman, Justin Schlosberg and Lina Dencik (2020), and *Democratic Delusions: How the Media Hollowed out Democracy and What We Can Do About It* (2024).

Des Freedman is Professor of Media and Communications at Goldsmiths and author of several books including *The Politics of Media Policy* (2008), *The Contradictions of Media Power* (2014), and *Misunderstanding the Internet* (with James Curran and Natalie Fenton) (2016). He has edited books on media reform, media and terrorism, liberalism and the political culture of the *Guardian*. He is a founding member of the UK Media Reform Coalition.

Jonathan Hardy is Professor of Communications and Media at the University of the Arts London. His books include *Sponsored Editorial Content in Digital Journalism* (editor, 2023), *Branded Content: The Fateful Merging of Media and Marketing* (2022), *Critical Political Economy of the Media* (2014), *Cross-Media Promotion* (2010), and *Western Media Systems* (2008). He is co-editor of *The Advertising Handbook* (2018/2011) and book series editor of *Routledge Critical Advertising Studies*. He is Principal Investigator for the Branded Content Governance Project 2022–25 (ESRC/AHRC ES/W007991/1).

Kaori Hayashi is a scholar of media and journalism in Japan and serves as Professor of Media and Journalism Studies at the Graduate School of Interdisciplinary Information Studies of the University of Tokyo. She is also Executive Vice President of the university, in charge of global and diversity affairs. She is also a contributor and columnist for a variety of mainstream media including Kyodo News Agency, Nikkei Women, Asahi Shimbun, one of the largest national dailies in Japan.

Michael Klontzas is based at Goldsmiths, University of London and is managing editor of the *Journal of Digital Media & Policy*. His research interests, publications and teaching are centred on media policy and technological innovation in the context of UK and European public service communications.

Winston Mano is Professor and a member of the University of Westminster's Communication and Media Research Institute (CAMRI). He is also a Course Leader for the MA in Media and Development and the Founder/Editor-in-Chief of the *Journal of African Media Studies*. Mano is also a Senior Research Fellow at the University of Johannesburg, South Africa. Mano joined CAMRI from the University of Zimbabwe in 2000.

L. Lusike Mukhongo is Associate Professor in the School of Communication at Western Michigan University. She has experience researching participatory digital cultures, global media and mobile technologies and is a recipient of various research awards and fellowships. She is also a member of several professional associations, such as the International Association of Media and Communication Research (IAMCR), the National Communication Association (NCA), and the Association of Internet Researchers (AOIR).

Graham Murdock, Emeritus Professor of Culture and Economy at Loughborough University, has published widely in the sociology and political economy of culture and communications. He has held visiting professorships at the Universities of Auckland, California at San Diego, Mexico City, Curtin, Bergen, the Free University of Brussels, and Stockholm and is currently Guest Professor at Fudan University in Shanghai. His work has been translated into 21 languages. Recent books include, as co-editor: *Money Talks: Media, Markets, Crisis* (2015), *New Media and Metropolitan Life: Connecting, Consuming, Creating* (in Chinese) (2015), *Carbon Capitalism and Communication: Confronting Climate Change* (2017) and a greatly expanded third edition of the influential text *Researching Communications* written jointly with colleagues (2021).

Tom O'Malley is Emeritus Professor of Media, Aberystwyth University and writes on press and broadcasting history. His publications include: *Closedown? The BBC and Government Broadcasting Policy,*

1979–1992 (1994); with Clive Soley, *Regulating The Press* (2000); with David Barlow and Phillip Mitchell, *The Media in Wales* (2005); with Janet Jones (Eds.) *The Peacock Committee and UK Broadcasting Policy* (2009); with Siân Nicholas (Eds.) *Moral Panics, Social Fears, and the Media* (2013) and *Newspapers, War and Society in the 20th Century* (2019). He co-founded the journal *Media History* and is currently completing a study of the UK press in World War II.

Vibodh Parthasarathi maintains a multidisciplinary interest in media policy, digital transitions and policy literacy. Associate Professor at the Centre for Culture, Media and Governance at Jamia Millia Islamia, New Delhi, he has been a visiting scholar at the University of Queensland, KU Leuven, University of Helsinki, and IIT Bombay. Parthasarathi has been at the forefront of media policy research in India and a winner of numerous grants including from the Ford Foundation, Canada's IDRC, SSRC, and University Grants Commission. His classroom initiatives at project-based learning in media policy have been put together in *Pedagogy in Practice* (2022).

John Durham Peters is María Rosa Menocal of English and Professor of Film and Media Studies at Yale University. He is the author of *Speaking into the Air: A History of the Idea of Communication* (1999), *Courting the Abyss: Free Speech and Liberal Tradition* (2005), *The Marvelous Clouds: Toward a Philosophy of Elemental Media* (2015), and, most recently, *Promiscuous Knowledge: Information, Image, and Other Truth Games in History* (2020), co-authored with the late Kenneth Cmiel, as well as numerous essays and articles.

Victor Pickard is the C. Edwin Baker Professor of Media Policy and Political Economy at the University of Pennsylvania's Annenberg School for Communication, where he co-directs the Media, Inequality & Change (MIC) Center. Pickard's research focuses on media history, media activism and the politics and normative foundations of media policy. He has published more than 150 articles and essays and his public writings have appeared in outlets such as *the Guardian, the Washington Post, Jacobin,* and *the Nation.* He has authored or edited six books, including the award-winning monographs *America's Battle for Media Democracy* and *Democracy Without Journalism?*

Nelson Ribeiro is Professor of Communication Studies at the Catholic University of Portugal where he is the Dean of the Faculty of Human Sciences and Director of the Lisbon Winter School for the Study of Communication (co-organised with Barbie Zelizer). Chair of the History Section at the International Association for Media and Communication Research (IAMCR), he is a co-author of *The Wireless World: Global Histories of International Radio Broadcasting* (2022). His most recent works focus on colonial broadcasting, radio and public diplomacy and the history of disinformation.

Naomi Sakr is Professor Emerita of Media Policy at the Communication and Media Research Institute (CAMRI), University of Westminster, where her research focuses on the international political economy of media in Arab countries, looking at governance, production and distribution. She has written three books, co-authored one, edited two and co-edited two and published more than 20 articles in refereed journals. Within her specialisation she has worked on media law, management and sustainability, journalism and human rights, children's media, women's media activism and developments in the medium of television.

Jean Seaton has written about conflict (*The Media of Conflict*; *Carnage and the Media*), was recently an advisor for *Northern Ireland: Living with the Troubles* at the IWM and worked on the media and politics. Her volume of the official history of the BBC is *'Pinkoes and Traitors': The BBC and the Nation*. With James Curran, she is author of *Power Without Responsibility*, 9th edition (2024). She is Director of the Orwell Foundation which awards prizes for political journalism and writing and a member of the British Broadcasting Challenge which works for an open discussion of the future of broadcasting.

Klaus Unterberger is Head of the Public Value Department at Austrian Broadcasting Corporation (ORF), focusing on its public service mission and remit, in charge of substantial elements of ORF's quality control system, relevant scientific research, internal and external communications, and international cooperation. As host of ORF TV programme *Dialogforum*, he focuses on the public debate of quality journalism of public service media. He is one of the initiators of the international Public Service Internet Manifesto. Representing its management, he is member of the Board of Ethics of ORF.

Leo Watkins is a PhD student in Media and Communications at Goldsmiths, University of London researching the national press and the rise of the New Right in 1970s and 1980s Britain. He was the lead author on the UK study for the Centre for Media, Data and Society's Media Influence Matrix project. He has been a member of the Media Reform Coalition's coordinating committee.

Dwayne R. Winseck is a Professor at the School of Journalism and Communication, with a cross appointment to the Institute of Political Economy, Carleton University, Ottawa, Canada. His research interests include the political economy of communications, communications and media history, theory, policy and regulation. He is also the Director of the Social Sciences and Humanities Research Council funded Global Media and Internet Concentration Project which brings together 50 scholars studying the structure and evolution of the communications, internet and media industries in 40 countries from 1984 until the present. The project started in 2021 and will run until 2028.

Sally Young is Professor of Australian Politics and Media at the University of Melbourne. She is the author of the award-winning book *Paper Emperors: The Rise of Australia's Newspaper Empires* (2019), as well as its sequel, *Media Monsters* (2023) which reveals how those empires transformed into a handful of powerful companies between 1941 and 1972. She has also published books on election reporting, press photography, political advertising and government communication.

INDEX